Polish Your People Skills

Bobbi Linkemer

AMACOM NEW MEDIA
American Management Association

New York • Atlanta • Boston • Chicago • Kansas City • San Francisco • Washington, D.C.
Brussels • Mexico City • Tokyo • Toronto

*Library of Congress Cataloging-in-Publication Data
   Linkemer, Bobbi.
     Polish your people skills / Bobbi Linkemer.
        p.   cm.
     Includes index.
     ISBN 1-890003-03-4
        1. Psychology, Industrial.   2. Organizational behavior.
     3. Interpersonal communication.   I. Title.
     HF5548.8.L53   1998
     158.7—dc21   98-34030
                                                            CIP*

*Printing number
10   9   8   7   6   5   4   3   2   1*

Contents

Introduction

Organizations, no matter what their size or SIC code, no matter how technologically advanced or automated they may be, all depend on the human element to keep them in business. After all, organizations are staffed by people, managed by people, provide financial remuneration and other rewards to people, and ultimately serve people through their products or services. *Polish Your People Skills* is about getting along with the people you encounter in your workplace, developing constructive relationships, and learning to deal effectively with all of the obstacles that can trip you up as you try to do the first two.

You have so much more control over the quality of your interactions with others than you may realize. The first thing you can control is your *attitude.* Sometimes all it takes is a little attitude adjustment to prevent a problem, mend a mess, or find a new friend who may have been there all along. The second thing within your control is *what you say and how you say it.* Regardless of the content of any message, it is mostly the *delivery* that counts. The third thing you can control is your own *sincere desire to develop and enhance the interpersonal skills* that make it possible to get along with anyone, any time, in any situation.

Polish Your People Skills deals with all three of these elements, but particularly with developing and enhancing your interpersonal skills. The book is divided into three sections. The first, "Creating Positive Relationships," will help you create balance in your busy life, learn the importance and nuts and bolts of teamwork, and lay the foundation for all sound relationships: trust. It also looks at the important role communication plays in getting along with people and what it takes to work things out with an opponent so that both of you come out winners.

In Section Two, "Dealing with Difficult Situations," the emphasis shifts to your work environment and the conditions with which you live each day. Every organization has a "personality," an identifiable culture all its own. After you get a feel for which of these cultures best describes your company, you will learn how to survive and thrive in some of the toughest of them.

Finally, Section Three, "Dealing with Difficult People," gets to the heart of what makes people tick and how you can use that understanding to diffuse potential problems and manage seemingly unmanageable relationships.

If you are holding this book in your hand and have gotten this far, you are in control of two critical factors already. You have a positive attitude and a sincere desire to acquire and strengthen your people skills. *Polish Your People Skills* is intended to help you achieve that goal, but the proof is in the practice. If you learn a new approach or new skills and just *think* about them, it isn't likely to change or improve anything. On the other hand, if you try to incorporate what you've learned into your behavior or test it in the real world, you make it yours; and that can change everything.

Good luck and good reading!

SECTION ONE
Creating Positive Relationships

CHAPTER ONE

Putting Your Job in Perspective

Paula Slayden's life is a delicate balancing act in which she juggles a demanding job, a husband, and two small daughters. Her entire career, spanning 15 years, has been spent with one company. Along the way, she has graduated high school, attended college, married, started a family, and advanced through the ranks from a part-time, co-op, high school student to her current position as executive secretary to a vice-president of a Fortune 500 company.

Since I've been here, my entire life has changed—several times, in fact. When I started in 1983, I was a senior in high school in Alton, Illinois, working here part time. I worked for Alton Boxboard, which became Alton Packaging, which became Jefferson Smurfit Corporation. In 1986, while I was working in the personnel department, we acquired Container Corporation of America—a very big acquisition. I was ready for a change in 1990 and heard about a job as a secretary in the corporate office. I applied for it and was hired.

My first job at corporate was working for the vice president of the carton division, until he was promoted. Now, he is the president of the company. Then I worked for his successor; and, when *he* was promoted, he took me with him. Since I've been here, I've seen three presidents, the growth of this division, and the company go public, then private, then public again.

I still live in Illinois and commute thirty-three miles each way. I don't mind the commute. In fact, I find it's a good way to wind down before I get home, especially if I've had a bad day or I'm stressed out. It's about an hour coming in and forty-five to fifty minutes going home, which makes it an eleven-hour day.

I've been married for twelve and a half years. I have two children, both girls, a seven-year-old and twenty-month-old. I'm really lucky when it comes to child care. My family lives in the area, and my husband's job makes it possible for him to take care of the children every afternoon and all day on Mondays. Our mothers pitch in the rest of the time. My husband is a great dad. He has always taken care of them. In fact, he has the kids more than I do, which really makes me sad sometimes.

With the first baby, I went right back to work. With the second one, I took three months off. I did have a sitter lined up the second time, but after a month she quit. I had been out three months, had it all arranged, and then it unraveled. My mom volunteered to take care of the baby, which really eased my mind.

I do have a good support system. I wonder sometimes how I could do it without that. At home and here at work I try to be proactive, to anticipate what might come up. It takes a *lot of planning.* My day starts the night before. I feel that the minute I get home I'm already starting on the next day—helping with homework, getting clothes set out, and attending to 100 details. While I'm taking my bath, I'm thinking: *O.K., I've got to do this, this, and this.* Sometimes, my mind just doesn't shut off.

If I don't do that, the whole next morning falls apart. On Mondays, I think I can slack off because my husband is home, but I really can't. We have this little routine every morning. If that routine gets messed up somehow, I get stressed; and, of course, it usually does get messed up. Either the garage door doesn't go up or one of the kids is sick or *something* goes wrong.

I've never thought of myself as a control freak; I'm just trying to be organized. At work, my desk is a mess, and I'm probably not the neatest person in the world. But I know where everything is. At home, my husband plays with the kids; so, when I walk in the door, the place is a disaster. But I'd rather have him playing with them than come home to a perfect house. I do try to get things picked up before I go to bed at night, but I'm not compulsive about dust and neatness. Our house isn't huge, but it is warm and friendly.

I take my job seriously. I take responsibility for it, and I want to do it well, no matter what the task. But I believe that no matter who I work for, I can't put myself up there too high. I realize that I work for a very important person in my company, but I try hard not to use his power or to be too aggressive when I'm asking for something on his behalf. I know how that feels, because I've been on the receiving end of those requests in the past.

I am an emotional person. I let things get to me, though I've learned to suppress that somewhat. If things aren't going well, it's usually more of a personal issue than a job-related one. When it involves another person, I try to step back and think, *Why am I letting myself get upset about this? I know I can't change that person. Maybe he's having a bad moment or a bad day.* I tell myself to stop exerting so much effort worrying about making things right with him, and just do my job the best way I can. I try not to take it home and let it affect my attitude there. The drive home helps me shift gears into my "going-home mood."

I was seventeen years old when I started working for this company, and I've had to do a lot of growing up. Over the years, I've learned two important lessons: *Don't take things personally,* and *don't burn bridges.*

* * *

Working is a consuming activity—time-consuming, mind-consuming, and energy-consuming. If you work in an office, chances are your mind starts racing the minute you hit the door. If you have a family, it probably never stops racing. Only the subject changes between home and work. Like Paula Slayden's, your life requires *a lot of planning* and seems like a never-ending cycle of planning, doing, planning, and more doing. If you commute, as Paula does, your time on the road or on some form of public transportation may be the *only* time you have to unfrazzle your nerves and switch gears.

For people with careers and families, life often seems like a juggling act with far too many plates in the air. The problem, of course, is striking a balance among all those plates so that the really important ones don't come crashing to the floor and create a mess for you to clean up before you start juggling them all over again.

To balance means to hold in a state of equilibrium, to harmonize, or to compare and evaluate the relative importance of several elements. To balance one's life means to apply all of those definitions to the numerous roles and responsibilities you face each day. Only then will you be able to put your job in any meaningful perspective.

What Matters Most

Let us assume that your life is much like other people's lives in that you are trying to achieve some semblance of equilibrium. Your job is important to you. Your family depends on you. Your parents are getting older, and you can already see how their needs are changing. You would like to spend more time with friends. You are committed to your church or synagogue or other place of worship. You care about your community, and you want to give something back to the world in which you live.

As you deal with all those pulls and tugs on your time, if you have the feeling that someone or something is getting lost in the shuffle, it may be *you.* If you can't remember the last time you went to a museum or took a walk in the park or just sat and did absolutely nothing and, if the last book you bought yourself was *Meditations for Women Who Do Too Much,* it is time to take a break and take stock.

How and where would you begin to compare and evaluate the relative importance of all of the elements in your life, when they all seem equally important? Where would you find the extra time to cram in one more obligation? Before you rush out and take a course on time management, consider that it may be *your life* you should be managing, rather than your time. After all, everyone gets the same number of hours and minutes each day to work with—no more, no less. Why, then, do some people seem to walk purposefully through the demands of life, while others look as if they are failing a stress test on a runaway tread mill?

If you are the latter, the difference may be the absence of a sense of purpose in your life. If you have a definable purpose, everything you do moves you in the direction of fulfilling it. Purpose has a two-fold function: First, it acts as a compass, always keeping you headed in the right direction; and, second, it is a gyroscope, keeping you level and balanced. If you don't have purpose in your life, you are like a rudderless boat, drifting along in whatever direction the wind carries you, feeling out of control and at the mercy of the storms of life. Companies that operate without a purpose often drift right out of business; people who operate that way tend to sail directly into chaos.

When a company drifts off course, or has never set a course to begin with, the solution often is to write a company mission. A mission answers these questions: Why are we in business? What is our purpose? What is it that were trying to accomplish? It makes very good sense for people to adopt a similar approach; and, indeed, every good time/life management program advocates just that as a starting point.

When was the last time you contemplated such questions in terms of your own life? If it has been a while, or if you have never done it, why not do it now? Writing a personal mission, as you probably guessed, is a little more complicated than just sitting down and dashing one off in your spare time. Take the time, *make* the time to go off somewhere and *really think* about what is important to you, what you value. This process will help you answer the question posed earlier: *How and where would you begin to compare and evaluate the relative importance of all of the elements in your life, when they all seem equally important?*

A good way to start is to make a list of all the roles you play in your life. Divide a piece of paper in half. On the left side, list your roles: parent, son or daughter, spouse, employee, member of some organized religion, volunteer in your community, Girl Scout leader or softball coach, and anything else of significance. On the right side of the page, write down what you would like to achieve in each of these areas. Then look over your two-column list. You will probably find a fairly comprehensive picture of what is important to you. This becomes the basis of your personal mission statement.

Your Relationship With Yourself

If you're not comfortable with the concept of roles, reflect on the *relationships* in your life and what you hope to achieve within each one of them while you are alive. To kick start your ability to do this, some experts suggest that you picture your own funeral (this is not as depressing as it sounds) and listen to each important person in your life express how he or she remembers you. That's the most direct route to discovering who and what matters most to you.

When you begin to explore your relationships, why not begin with the most important and most overlooked relationship you have—the one with *yourself?* To break it down even further, ask yourself what you would like to achieve physically, mentally, emotionally, socially, and spiritually. After all, if you neglect this critical relationship, the rest of them will suffer as a consequence.

If you are stressed out of your mind, sick, or so overwhelmed that you never nurture yourself in even the smallest way, not only will this relationship fall apart, so will you. One way or another, you will simply unravel. There is too much reliable evidence to support the mind-body connection to ignore the consequences of self-neglect.

Your Physical Side

Since most people think of themselves in terms of their bodies, let's start there. Physically, what matters to you? What do you want for yourself in terms of your physical well-being, health, level of fitness, and appearance? The answers to these questions will be uniquely your own because no two people want the same things. At the very least, you probably desire an absence of illness; and, at the very most, you may aspire to optimum wellness and vitality.

Try to be very specific when you describe what is important to you in every area of your relationship with yourself. What does physical well-being mean to you? Be spontaneous and even wordy if you have to. You'll go back to this later and pull out the essence of what you are writing now, so just let it flow.

If fitness is part of your physical picture, what would it take to consider yourself fit? Would it be how far or how long you can jog or swim or hike? How much or how little you weigh? How many hours' sleep you need at night? The number of situps or pushups you can do? How much weight you can lift or how many repetitions you can achieve?

In terms of appearance, try to be realistic. If you are a five-foot-two-inch, fifty-year-old, graying brunette woman, it is not very realistic to set a goal of being a five-foot-seven-inch, thirty-five-year-old redhead. Well, the redhead part you could achieve; but the rest is doubtful. If your weight or size matter, include them; but again, stay grounded in reality. Few women look like Cindy Crawford, and fewer men would ever make the cover of *Muscle and Fitness* magazine.

Your Mental/Intellectual Side

We are a "thinking culture," and much of our lives is lived in our heads. We plan, we remember, we think about what we've done that we wish we could do over again, we analyze, we ruminate, we go around in mental circles. Try *not* thinking for even a minute. It is very difficult. The stream of thoughts that goes through your mind is usually more like a torrent, rushing, falling all over itself, as out of control as riding the rapids. Many meditation practices revolve around observing one's thoughts and trying to still the mind. It is not easy to do.

At least part of all that thinking involves taking in, processing, integrating, and using information. Minds are for learning, and in your job, you have plenty of opportunity to use the intellectual side of your minds. The questions to ask yourself here are about how you want to feed your mind, expand your mind, and use your mind. What interests you? What would you like to learn? What books have you wanted to read but never had the time or the discipline to follow through on your intentions? Do you need more training or education to get ahead in your career? In what area? In other words, what matters to you in the intellectual realm of your life? What are your aspirations? Write them down.

Your Emotional Side

While the philosopher René Descartes is best remembered for one line, "I think, therefore I am," he might just as well have observed, "I feel, therefore I am." People are emotional beings, and we can run the gamut from euphoric to despondent, often in the space of minutes. Is your emotional life what you would like it to be? Are you happy, content, at peace with yourself—or somewhere between vaguely discontented and downright depressed?

Obviously, you have neither the time nor the training to conduct self-therapy in this section of your exploration, but certainly you know how you feel now versus how you want to feel. You know if you are lonely or sad or content, just as you know if you are experiencing emotional discomfort or equanimity. You don't have to be a psychotherapist to ask yourself, *How do I feel at this moment? Is this how I want to feel? If not, what would I prefer?*

Your Social Side

Just as you need a relationship with yourself, you also need others in your life. Few things are more fulfilling than having friends to call on when you want a shoulder to cry on or someone to laugh with. Are you enjoying quality of friendships? Or are your "friends" really only acquaintances of convenience? Have you formed genuine relationships in your workplace? Do you want to, or are you guarded in this environment? Perhaps most the most important questions you can ask yourself are these: *Am I having fun? Do I enjoy myself in the company of others, or do I hold back and just go through the motions?*

Social life is a complex topic. It involves all the things you do with your own time, even if that time consists of only the brief moments between tasks, and the people with whom you choose to do those things. For many people, being social involves a husband, a wife, or a significant other. When you think about your social life, you may instantly convert that thought to how your love life is going.

How *is* it going? Do you have a special person in your life? Are you happy with that person, or is the relationship in trouble? If there is no such special person, how do you feel about that? Lonely? Unfulfilled? Content? Relieved? What *do* you have? What do you want? How do you picture yourself with others in the picture? Draw that picture in words.

Your Spiritual Side

"When people are buffeted about by change, the need for spiritual belief intensifies," observed authors John Naisbitt and Patricia Aburdene in *Megatrends 2000,* a book that predicted the trends of the nineties. "At the dawn of the third millennium," wrote Naisbitt and Aburdene, "there are unmistakable signs of a worldwide multi-denomination religious revival." This revival is taking many forms here in the West. While traditional and fundamental religions are thriving, many Americans are turning away from organized religion to everything from New Age thought to such Eastern spiritual practices as yoga and meditation.

Whatever scenario describes you, your spiritual life is worthy of inclusion in this personal inventory. Are you comfortable in your faith, or are you still searching? Have you stayed with your original religion, ventured out into non-traditional beliefs, or simply dropped out? Again, the question is, Are you where you want to be? Have you found a path to walk, or are you lost in the woods without a map? Describe your destination in that right column.

Your Relationship With Your Work

The relationship that consumes more of your time than any other is the one you have with your job. Whether you think of it as just a job, your life's work, or your career, this is where you spend your physical and mental energy, as well as your prime time each day. Where does your work fit in your hierarchy of priorities? How do you feel about it? Would you describe it as a healthy relationship or a sick one? Are you spending your daylight hours as you would wish to, or are you living a life of quiet despair until your are released from "prison" each evening?

If you think of your work place as Alcatraz with no hope of parole, you don't need to be told you have a problem. The question is, What would you rather be doing? What does your ideal job look like? Is that picture a possibility or a pipe dream? Not that there is anything wrong with dreaming. As Goethe said, "If you can dream it, you can do it." But, like wanting to be thirty-five when you are fifty or five feet seven inches when it just isn't possible, yearning to be a opera singer when you can't carry a tune, is more of a fantasy than a dream.

Few areas in your life are more important than your relationship with your work, and few require such investigation to set right whatever you feel is wrong. Finding the work that is right for you would require a book of its own; but, for the purposes of your mission statement, start by writing down the work you would like to be doing and the contribution you feel you could make if you did it. What does a job or a career mean to you? Do you work to live or live to work? Do you know the difference? How will your dream job differ from the one you have now? Why would it be better? What do you want to gain from the work you do? How high a priority is this to you?

Your Relationship With Your Spouse or Significant Other

No matter what the statistics may tell us about how many single people there are in this country, it still seems that it is a couple's world, with everybody marching two-by-two like Noah's Ark. The fairy tales of love we heard during our childhood stopped at the end of the wedding ceremony and the beginning of a life to be lived happily ever after; but life does go on, as anyone who has been married well knows. Today, there are even more strains on marriages than ever before, especially when both partners work, juggle demanding schedules, take turns parenting, care for aging parents, and try to get their own needs sandwiched in between those of everyone else.

If you are in a committed relationship, married or not, you know how hard it is to carve out quality time to be with your partner. Yet, if this relationship is important to you, it is worth all the effort you can give it. Assuming you are married or the equivalent, are you satisfied with the way things are going, or would you design it differently if you had the chance? Working through your personal mission gives you that chance. Describe how you would like it to be in the best of all possible worlds. What should change? What *can* change? What will it take to change it?

While couplehood takes effort, so does becoming part of a couple if you happen to be going solo at the moment. Dating at any age or stage of life can range from delightful to dreary to dreadful, depending on the circumstances. Meeting people you want to date, suffering through those evenings from hell, finding and losing love, or getting involved with Mr. or Ms. Wrong are only a few of the pitfalls. On the other hand, finding a new relationship is exciting, getting to know another person is intriguing, and falling in love is … well, you know how lovely that can be.

If you are open to a relationship, but not in the right one for you, what would the right one look like? What do you want? What do you *not* want? Could you paint a word picture of your ideal, healthy, mutually satisfying, and growth-promoting relationship? Try it right here and right now.

Your Relationship With Your Children

Children are demanding, and one thing you can count on them to demand is a top position on any priority list. They need care and nurturing, especially when they are sick. They need guidance, consistency, and discipline. They need someone to drive car pool; someone to keep them in clean, peer-approved clothes; someone to help with homework. They need role models, helping hands, and soft shoulders. They need you all the time, or so it seems.

If you are a working parent, the conflict in your responsibilities is something with which you are very familiar. You have pressures, obligations, and demands at work. You have all the same things at home. Which of these comes first? How do you decide? How do you create a balance? And, if you are a single, working parent, when and how do you get some relief from your twenty-four-hour-day marathon life? What kind of parent do you hope to be? What do you want to achieve with and for your children? Try to capture those feelings in words.

Your Relationship With Your Family and Friends

Then, of course, there are the other very important people in your life: your parents, your family and extended family, and the friends you treasure. You need them; they need you. You are busy; they are busy. Yet, they must go somewhere on your list. How do you find time for each other? How do you summon up the energy to be a care-giver if someone is ill, aging, totally dependent, or just plain in need of your understanding?

You may have no idea where or how; but the minute you are called upon to do any of those things, it's amazing how you find the necessary time, energy, compassion, or whatever else is required to resolve the situation. What would you like your friends and relatives to say about you at your one hundredth birthday? (Sometimes that's easier than conjuring up the image of your own funeral.) What you would want them to say is what you would hope to achieve in these precious relationships.

Your Relationship With Your Community

Unless you live on an uninhabited island somewhere, you are part of a larger community; and, consciously or unconsciously, you have a relationship with that community. How you maintain your home and lawn, the way you interact with the check-out clerk at the grocery store and the letter carrier who delivers your mail, whether or not you clean up after your pet, for whom you vote in local elections, your consideration or lack of it for your neighbors, and an almost endless list of other ways in which you affect those around you are all threads in this relationship.

If you extend the sense of community out in all directions, you will see that these same attitudes have an impact not only on your neighbors but on people you don't know, may never meet, and have never heard of. As the world gets smaller, your effect on others gets bigger. What you do and say has implications that go beyond your imagination.

How would you have that relationship look? What effect would you like to have? What difference do you want to make? What good do you want to bring to your neighbors—

nearby or across an ocean? What does a citizen of the world look like to you?

Your Relationship With the Planet

There is another meaning to the phrase *citizen of the world* that refers to your relationship with the planet earth. It is said that when a butterfly flaps its wings on one side of the world, it creates a tidal wave on the other side. Nothing exists in a vacuum; everything that happens affects everything else. Quantum physicists will tell you that the observer of an event influences that event as much as the event influences the observer. Buddhism teaches that everything is interconnected in a series of flowing processes, constantly changing. Nothing is static; nothing is separate. Everything is part of the whole.

If these scientific and spiritual teachings are to be believed, we have a great responsibility to our host planet. What kind of a citizen of the world are you? If you have never thought about it, this is a good time to do so. Do you generate unnecessary waste? Do you recycle? Are you a conspicuous consumer of natural resources? Do you think "green" and buy "green"? Do you see the earth as a living, breathing organism or as a pile of rock? What would you change if you could (which, of course, you can)? Describe what you would do. Then, do it.

Putting It All together

Assuming you actually answered all of these questions, you probably have writer's cramp and a very strong sense of how you want to function within each of these relationships. Now is the time to go mining for the gold among all those words.

Distill them to their essence—one or two lines about each relationship. Write each part of your personal mission statement in present-tense affirmations. What follows is an example of what such a distillation of your thoughts might look like.

Mission

In my relationship with *myself,* I am vibrantly healthy, alive, and in harmony with my body, mind, and spirit. I strive to become all I am capable of being; yet, I forgive and accept myself when I am less than perfect.

In my relationship to *my job,* I am fully engaged in work I love, for which I am appreciated and well-paid. Wherever possible, I use my talents and training to benefit others in some way.

In my relationship with *my spouse or significant other,* I am a full and equal partner in our life together, contributing, sharing, and communicating with openness.

In my relationship with *my children,* I foster their growth and create an environment in which they can grow and achieve their fullest potential as autonomous human beings.

In my relationship with *my family and friends,* I make time for them; I listen to them; I support them; and, as often as possible, I have fun with them.

In my relationship with *my community,* I am a good neighbor who contributes where and when I am able to. I accept and value the differences among people, yet remain aware of the many things we have in common.

In my relationship with *the earth,* I remain conscious that this living planet was once perfect and unspoiled. Thus, I make every effort to preserve and protect its life for the next generation and to leave it just a little better than I found it.

Conclusion

Crafting a personal mission statement takes time and thought. It is definitely hard work. So, why do it? You do it because it defines your purpose; it guides your progress; and it is the standard against which you can evaluate your decisions, your behavior, and your allocation of time and energy. Your priorities will no longer be a mystery to you. When faced with choices, you will have some sound basis for making them.

For example, if you value being *vibrantly healthy, alive, and in harmony with your body,* you will make it a top priority to exercise, eat the right foods, and get adequate sleep. You will know those things are important to you, so you will find a way to do them. If you have decided that you want to help preserve a planet that is being raped, ravaged, and polluted, you will make the effort to conserve, to recycle, and to be mindful about how you treat the earth.

Will having a personal mission statement make your juggling act a snap and prevent the plates you're keeping in the air from crashing to the ground? Unfortunately, the answer is *no.* A mission statement will not solve every problem you have in terms of time and life management. But it most certainly *will* help you create a sense of equilibrium in your life, bring some order to your priority list, and help you put your relationship with your job in its proper perspective.

CHAPTER TWO

Developing People Skills

Annie Biggs is one of the top hair stylists at Salon VIP in Chesterfield, Missouri. Ten years into her career, she is talented, professional, and totally "client-focused." She is well-liked by coworkers, management, and especially her clients, who book their appointments months in advance to be sure they are on her schedule. No one gives a better haircut or does more magic with color than she does. But, most important, no one can make a client feel quite as important or as beautiful as Annie can.

I've been at this salon three years, at the last one for six years, and at my first job for one year. Every salon is different. The first shop I worked in was commission-based, and we rented space. We were independent business people who didn't actually work together. If there was competition there, I didn't experience it because I was brand new and didn't have any clients yet. But I did know I was miserable there, so I called my beauty school instructor and asked if she knew of any good places to work. She referred me to a guy named Dennis at a shop called *Friends.* Four interviews later, I started working there.

It was different from the first place I worked because it was salary-based and provided lots of good benefits. That was very unusual. The people who worked there weren't competitive because they were on salary. We did work together. We bounced ideas off of each other. Nobody had a *I'm-better-than-you* attitude. We were all equal, and there was a total sense of being part of a team. The boss really cared about our input. We had monthly meetings, where we closed down the shop on the first Tuesday of every month for an hour during the day and talked about how things were going.

I formed a lot of friendships there; many of them are still strong. A lot of that had to do with the fact that we were all about the same age and so much alike. Everybody was very happy there. I was happy up to the end. Dennis left to open this shop, and I left too because I thought this was a great opportunity. Most of my friends moved here with us. I would have been so unhappy if I had stayed there without them.

We all have a similar work ethic here. The client is number one, and our continuing education is number two. We all are interested in going to classes, and we help each other out. One of the stylists hurt her finger and can't get it wet for a couple of days. She can't work, so we are trying to get her clients done for her. At most salons, people wouldn't do that. She won't make any money, but she doesn't care. She just wants her customers to be happy.

We are friends, so no one would ever do anything to hurt anyone else, like going after their clients. That does happen in some salons. We wouldn't dream of doing that to each other. If one of my clients switches to another stylist, that's O.K. with me. I'm glad she's still coming to the salon. I would rather have a customer switch than go somewhere else.

It's important to get along with people you work with, and that is especially true here because we are stuck in one spot all day. While we do interact with the people around us, we certainly don't stand around talking to each other about personal stuff. We include the client in the conversations, and it's all very natural.

I've heard it said that being a good hair stylist is 10 percent skill and 90 percent knowing how to talk to people. To maintain good client relationships, I've learned to keep my personal life at home and to concentrate on the person in my chair. The client isn't paying money to hear my life story. Even if he or she asks, it doesn't mean that person wants to hear every single detail of my life. On the other hand, I *do* hear the life stories of many of my clients. I just listen and try to give advice if I have any.

As far as being able to relate to so many different kinds of clients, I think it's because I grew up in a lot of different places and knew a lot of different people. My father was in the military, so we moved around a lot. I spent my summers in New Jersey and the rest of year in Missouri when I was a kid, so I had two different sets of friends. Also, with my mom being handicapped, I really know what stress is. When I hear all these stories about how horrible life is, sometimes I think, they don't *know* what real stress is.

Everybody has to deal with people they don't like. I like 90 percent of my clients; but I treat them all exactly the same, no matter how I feel. The best part of what I do is that it's never boring; it's always something different. Even though the job itself is pretty much the same, day after day, everybody's hair is different and everybody's personality is different. It's just fun to have variety because I have a tendency to get bored very easily. I think if I sat at a desk all day I would go nuts. Here, there is always something going on. I've formed some real friendships with clients and even have a few outside-of-work relationships with them and their husbands.

The worst thing about this job is that I can never wake up and have a bad day. I can't say to people, *I'm in a bad mood, so leave me alone.* I can't pull my back out and stay home. I can't just push paper away, because I have fourteen or fifteen humans to reschedule and take care of. But, other than the fact that it's grueling, I really do love what I do.

*   *   *

Wherever you work and whatever you do, unless you are the only person in your work environment and you never encounter another human being, you are bound to find yourself working with others. It is simply an unavoidable fact of life. It is people, after all, who own businesses, run them, work in them, and buy their products or services. Consider these familiar statements: Our *employees* are our most important resource. We are in business to serve our *customers.* The most important goal of the company is to provide our *shareholders* with a healthy return on their investment.

Employees, customers, and shareholders obviously are people; and, if we are to believe these three assertions, they are very important people. Yet, if there is a single area where most of us have deficiencies and receive little or no training to correct them, it is in the area of "people skills." Look around your own office and notice all the things that needlessly go wrong between people—tense situations, muddled communication, put downs, hurt feelings, poor management, sarcastic remarks, silent resentments, power plays, one-upmanship, secrecy, gossip, and so on.

These things take place, not only where you work, but everywhere. People's inability to deal effectively with others in the workplace, in the home, and in almost any setting is a sad commentary on our society. What is even sadder is that working and getting along with others is really not all that difficult. Every religious tradition addresses this issue in some way, and they all boil people skills down to little more than a sentence.

- Do unto others as you would have them do unto you.
- What unites all people is the desire to be happy.
- Do not judge another until you have walked a mile in his moccasins.
- Gentleness overcomes rigidity; when it confronts a wall of stone, the power of water prevails.

Could such simple concepts work in the real world? Can they be put to practical use in your everyday life, particularly your work life? Are human relations really as simple as they make it appear? The answer is *yes*.

Words to Live By

Do unto others as you would have them do unto you is a line from the *New Testament* that most people have heard at one time or another in their lives. You may know it as the "Golden Rule." What is interesting about it is that it is actually based on a far older teaching from the *Old Testament*, which was worded: *Do not treat others as you would not wish to be treated.* The different is subtle. The first seems more positive than the second, but it is actually more difficult to put into practice.

Think about any adversarial situation in which you might find yourself and what it would take to figure out, first, what *you* would want if you were in the other person's shoes, and, second, to behave as you would hope the other person might under similar circumstances. It's tough, especially if you are experiencing strong emotions at that time.

On the other hand, the simple prohibition of *not* striking out with harsh words or belligerent behavior is something you might be able to do. Picture the same scene. Perhaps a coworker has made a mistake that affects your work and reflects badly on you. Your first impulse might be to voice your dismay and let that coworker have it, so to speak.

On the tip of your tongue could be something like, *Do you realize what you've done? How could you have been so stupid? I'm going to look like a complete idiot in front of my boss now because of you!* Perhaps that's a bit strong, but you get the idea. You're upset. In fact, you are downright angry. You want to let her know how much trouble her mistake is going to cause you. How do you make that little negative-sounding sentence work for you in the heat of a moment like this one?

You say to yourself, *Stop! Wait a minute.* And you take a deep breath. If *you* had made a mistake—and, let's face it, you have probably made one or two in your life—what is the *last* thing you would want to hear? How stupid you are? What damage you've done? Words that, once said, can never be taken back? If you're smart, you want none of the above. You may not know what you or your coworker would want, but you certainly know, instinctively, what you would *not* want.

So, don't do any of it. Don't strike out. Don't make that person feel any worse than he or she already feels. Don't say something you'll regret later. Can it be that simple? The answer, once again, is yes. *But it's so negative,* you may be thinking. Perhaps, but, for some reason, the things we know we should not do make more of an impression than the things we should do. A case in point: Did you know that eight of the Ten Commandments begin with the words *Thou shalt not?*

Back to Basics

Refraining from saying or doing what you would hope no one would say or do to you is a good start, but it is not the whole picture by any means. In a little book called *Everything I Need to Know I Learned in Kindergarten,* author Robert Fulgham revisited our earliest lessons and concluded that they still applied, even in today's business world. For five-year-olds, learning to play nicely, to say *please* and *thank you,* and to share their belongings were tough lessons. As adults, many of us seem to have forgotten them.

The foundation upon which these lessons are built is thoughtful, respectful communication. Think about that for a moment. Behavior does not exist in a vacuum. Whatever you do, as it relates to another human being, is communicated in one of two ways: verbally or nonverbally. Often you are completely unaware of what or how you are communicating. What you say or do just seems to happen, spontaneously; and it doesn't always have the intended effect.

If you are someone who sincerely wants to do unto others as you would have them do unto you, but find that your good intentions sometimes fail to translate into the right words or actions, try going back to the basics of effective communication.

We all want to be acknowledged and valued. We want people to listen to us, to hear the meaning behind our words, to understand what we are saying. Yet, few of us *really listen* when others are speaking or observe the unspoken messages they convey through their body language and facial expressions. What we are lacking, it seems, are listening skills.

Try this simple exercise the next time you are engaged in a conversation, no matter how brief. Stop what you are doing, give your complete attention to the speaker, ask questions to get more information, and summarize in your own words what you heard to be sure you understood. Those are the most basic rules of effective listening.

When you are the person doing the talking, try this simple technique. Think of what you want to say in terms of five simple steps. Step one is setting up the conversation by explaining what you want to talk about and checking to see if the other person is willing to proceed. Is this a good time? Is she really present, or is she distracted or out of sorts?

If you sense it's O.K. to go on, step two is to get the other person's viewpoint *before* you offer yours. You may find this an unfamiliar and even uncomfortable way to converse, but step two is the key to respectful communication. Ask questions, and give her time to fully answer them. Check for understanding. That way, you'll get a handle on what she thinks, show her you are listening, and demonstrate that you do grasp her message.

When you have thoroughly listened to her point of view, step three is to express yours. Don't accuse or unintentionally attack by starting sentences with the word *you.* Rather, start them with *I,* as in *I think ...* or *I feel ...* or *my take on this is. ...*

Step four is to discuss the issue and to try to come to some agreement. This might only take a sentence or two.

Step five is to decide what to do next if anything has to be done. All of this can be accomplished in a matter of minutes. The important thing is not what the conversation is about but how you structure it. These five little steps are probably the most powerful communication skills you will ever learn.

Building Bridges

What unites all people is the desire to be happy is a Buddhist teaching that helps when you are having trouble dealing with a difficult person. If you can find nothing in common, no characteristic you can understand or accept, not a single thing about this person you can relate to, at least you know that you have one thing in common: Just because you are human, both of you want to be happy. In terms of a connection, it may not be much; but it is a place to start.

To negotiate, to arrive at some satisfactory compromise, you must find something you share, some way to build a bridge between you and the other person. Often that is quite easy. It can take less than a minute to find all sorts of common ground: gender, marital status and parenthood, employer, age, ethnic background, neighborhood, mutual friends, likes and dislikes, alma mater, place of worship, sports, hobbies, and many more. Any one or two will work to get you started.

The difficulty arises when you can find nothing. You have a problem with this person—opposing points of view, a personality conflict, differing agendas, something that clearly polarizes you. *Build a bridge? Are you kidding? We are from two different planets!* Even as such thoughts are going through your mind, you know both of you are from the same planet, are part of the same species, have the capacity to reason, and are seeking happiness. If that's all you find, that's where you begin because, unless you have the luxury of walking away and never seeing this person again, you have to begin somewhere.

What to Do About Differences

Finding a point of commonality is more important now than it has ever been. While there may have been differences in personality or education or style in the past, those differences pale in comparison to today's business environment.

The makeup of the American work force is vastly different than it was when most major corporations started in business. Where once we could look around and see a relatively homogeneous group of people, who were for the most part white and male, that is no longer the case. We are now seeing many more women, African-Americans, people from other countries and varied ethnic backgrounds, older adults, and people with disabilities.

What does that mean to you? It means you will be working side-by-side with a wide variety of people who, on the surface, are quite different from you and with whom you seem to have little in common. You may not understand them or the way they do things. They may not seem to fit in. You may have preconceived notions about them. You may even dislike them. But, ultimately, you will all have to work together. The work place is merely a microcosm of society, and it is an inescapable fact that society is becoming increasingly diverse.

Looking for connecting threads, no matter how fragile, is a first step in understanding your new coworkers and avoiding the destructive practice of stereotyping. All people have worth and dignity and deserve to be treated with respect. All people want pretty much the same things in life. All people have a right to work and provide for themselves and their families.

These are your first connecting threads. The rest will have to be carefully discovered or created. As the world gets smaller, your circle of associates will get larger. You can close your eyes and avoid the new reality, or you can open up to this opportunity to expand your horizons. There is much more to be gained from opening up.

Rush to Judgment

You may recognize this familiar line from the Native American tradition: *Do not judge another until you have walked a mile in his moccasins.* Like so many of their teachings, this one is based on respect. Native Americans are taught from childhood to respect their elders, the earth, the bounty of nature, and all living beings. Implicit in this teaching is the idea that judgment of others should be withheld unless one has walked another's path in life, experienced another's joy and pain, and felt what was in another's heart. A tall order? Of course, but also a great lesson in nonjudgmental acceptance and empathy.

How do you cultivate nonjudgmental acceptance in a society where everybody has an opinion about everything? These opinions are based on conditioning—input from countless sources we encounter on our own paths in life. The earliest opinions, of course, are from our parents and members of our immediate family. Sometimes they are spoken; sometimes we just sort of pick them up along long the way. Author and humorist Sam Levinson once observed that prejudice is transmitted not through the blood stream but through the stream of conversation in the home.

If your parents were staunch Republicans, chances are you are as well. If they liked certain kinds of foods and disliked others, your menu may not have changed very much over the years. Think of their religious preference, philosophy of child rearing, opinions of other family members, attitudes toward work, and how they dealt with people who were "not like them."

As your world grew, so did your exposure to an ever-widening circle of viewpoints and perspectives. Relatives, clergyman, teachers, friends, bosses, coworkers, and that big, catch-all category called "society" all contributed to your world-view. Then there were books and movies, newspapers and television, charismatic speakers, and chance encounters with strangers. You may not have any idea where most of your opinions originated or why you've hung on to them all these years. But they are there, stored in your mental file cabinet, waiting to be brought out into the world and attached to something or someone.

Imagine that a new woman has come into your department. You know absolutely nothing about her, except what you can observe. But you do have your stored data, which you immediately begin to apply. Based on what your first impressions trigger in your mind, you will form an instant opinion of this new person. You will give her either positive marks or negative ones, depending on your past experiences and the opinions you have developed along the way.

It is almost impossible to make no judgment at all, even if you genuinely try to keep an open mind. Years of conditioning and input from thousands of sources are coming together to color your judgment. In some ways, that is a good thing. If, every time you encountered something or someone new, you had to start from scratch with no back-up experience to draw on, you would probably go crazy. So the question is, How do you remain open to people and circumstances? How do you refrain from jumping to conclusions, putting them in pigeon holes, and assigning old labels that may not fit the new situation or person?

Making a Connection

Imagine for a moment that you have no preconceived notions, no old, worn-out opinions that may or may not fit the person you are meeting for the first time. Imagine, if it will help, that you are from a different planet. You know nothing. You are a blank slate to be filled in as you go along. With no preconceptions, no prejudices, no already formed opinions, you would really be quite open to getting to know someone. How would you go about it?

You would probably start by *looking* at the other person, which is the first thing most people do anyway. The important thing in this exercise is not to rush to judgment but to merely observe without labeling. The next step would be to *listen* for both content and meaning to what the person is saying. What is the message? What are the feelings behind the message? It's fine to ask questions, to inquire, all for the purpose of understanding. The third step would involve tuning in to what you *sense* from the nonverbal messages you are receiving.

These three steps will provide a first impression, which is not unusual. What *is* unusual is that you will not make a judgment based on that first impression. You will simply search for ways in which you are similar. Then you will step back and give this whole process some time. There will be second and third and fourth impressions, all of which will be opportunities to seek areas of commonality.

Each time you encounter this person will provide another chance to gather information. Of course, you will notice differences as well, because no two people are exactly alike. But your emphasis should be on how you are alike, not on how you differ from each other. The more links you find, the more you will begin to know this person. Eventually, you may even experience empathy—a true understanding of how he feels. That is the beginning of what it means "to walk a mile in his moccasins."

Life's Little Paradoxes

When it confronts a wall of stone, gentleness overcomes rigidity; the power of water prevails. This line may be less familiar than the first three. It is from one of many translations of a book called the *Tao Te Ching* or the *Way of Life,* written long ago in ancient China. This little book became the basis for an enduring spiritual tradition called Taoism. Like so many of its teachings, this one is a paradox. It means, by yielding, instead of fighting, we can overcome great obstacles. It is the underlying principle of the martial art, Tai Chi, and a good way to deal with force without resorting to more force.

If that doesn't seem to make sense, remember that Gandhi liberated an entire country with only two resources: three million determined people and the concept of passive resistance. Slowly and patiently, Gandhi's strategy of passive resistance got through to India's British oppressors and drove them out.

Similarly, Martin Luther King led the Civil Rights Movement in the 1960's, based on those same principles of nonviolence. Eventually, many unjust laws were changed and long-held practices of discrimination and segregation in this country began to break down.

There are those who argue that nonviolence could not possibly have worked against the ruthlessness of a tyrant like Hitler, but history would prove them wrong. In 1940, the Danes protested Nazi occupation of their country with social, political, and economic noncooperation, becoming one of the few countries to successfully resist all attempts to bring itself into Hitler's New Order. Perhaps the most dramatic example of "gentleness overcoming rigidity" occurred when the Nazis ordered all Danish Jews to wear the Star of David. The next day, virtually every Dane in the country, including the King, appeared in public with the yellow star conspicuously emblazoned on their sleeves.

Easy Does It

The point of all of these little historical vignettes is that fighting force with force is not the only way to accomplish what you want. Sometimes, in fact, it is the worst possible way. How could this possibly apply to your work situation? Think of how many times you have been on the receiving end of someone's bad temper, misused authority, or abusive behavior. Chances are your impulse has been to lash out and respond in kind. Of course, that isn't always possible. If it is your boss or someone in a position of power, you would be committing occupational suicide to strike back, even with a dirty look.

In such a case, what is your alternative? If you are like most people, you would probably swallow your anger and attempt to fake it until you could get away. This is hard on your poor adrenal glands, which are all geared up for unleashing the flight-or-fight response, not to mention the rest of your nervous system. If it isn't someone in authority, you may succumb to those impulses by turning on your heel and leaving or by lashing out—in other words, fighting force with force.

The other alternative is to pause a moment and remember that *gentleness overcomes rigidity.* Just once, don't flee; don't fight. Instead, try a nonviolent approach. It's not what people usually do because we all tend to experience a knee-jerk reaction to being attacked, verbally or any other way.

If you have the discipline to take a break—even a few seconds—between the attack and your response, that's all you will need to decide *how* you will respond. If you *don't* fight back, if you *don't* get angry, if you simply stay calm and reasonable, you may be very surprised at the results. Like water slowly eroding a rock, like Gandhi and Martin Luther King and the Danish people in wartime, you will eventually win the battle without resorting to undue force.

Conclusion

"People skills" may be a misnomer. Though it certainly does take skill to deal with people in the workplace, and any place, those skills must be built upon a foundation of respect—self-respect and respect for others. If you cultivate self-respect, you will want to be treated well and, thus, will treat others well. If you respect others, you will accept their differences and seek those things you have in common. If you respect others, you will try to get along, to understand where they are coming from, and to keep an open mind. If you respect others, you will not fight fire with fire, but will calmly refuse to be lured into potentially volatile situations.

As people, we all have problems of some kind. They may not be exactly alike, but chances are they are similar enough to develop some degree of understanding and empathy for another person. If, for example, you discover that one of your fellow workers has a sick child or an aging parent, or a spouse who has just been fired, and you have experienced any one of those problems, you will *know* just what that person is going through. With very little effort you will remember your pain and feel his. That is empathy. That is walking a mile in someone else's shoes.

CHAPTER THREE

Becoming a Team Player

Leslie Linkemer is a market manager for Anheuser Busch, Inc., responsible for five markets in the Florida Panhandle. From her first restaurant job at the age of sixteen to her present position with a Fortune 50 company, she has learned the importance of being a team player and of working collaboratively with others. That understanding, coupled with the skills she has developed over the years, has been a tremendous asset in building her successful career.

I started my career right out of college as a restaurant manager for a national restaurant chain. My first job was in Evansville, Indiana, which was followed by two other restaurants in St. Louis, Missouri. Each time I was promoted, and eventually I created my own position, regional marketing manager, in which I designed and executed marketing programs for seventy-two restaurants in eleven states.

I left the restaurant business to go to work for Carlsberg International, which was Anheuser Busch's import at the time. After three years in South Florida, where I worked with nine A-B wholesalers, I was hired into Anheuser-Busch as a market manager for the Florida panhandle. My present responsibilities require working with various sales teams to identify and capitalize on opportunities in the marketplace.

I've always considered myself a team player, and I would say that being one has played an important role in every step of my career path. I enjoy working with a team to get the job done, as opposed to doing it myself or trying to get someone else to do it. Throughout my career I've found that it is more effective to have more than one player on a team working to accomplish objectives.

I think being a team player has to do with the ability to take on different roles at different times. For example, if I am on a Process Improvement Team (PIT), sometimes I am a leader on that team; sometimes I am one of the people who interjects ideas and suggestions; and sometimes I am the scribe, taking the notes, organizing information, and helping everyone else put the pieces together.

I definitely think teams are effective. Right now, I'm on the Sales Team Advisory Roundtable (STAR), which is made up of people who are elected by our peers in each region and who come into St. Louis to address issues in the field. We send out a survey in advance asking for feedback. The responses run the gamut from sales to human resources and everything in between. The survey results are broken down into the most pressing concerns. We each choose the topic we want to tackle and volunteer to be on that team.

The reason these teams work so well is that they are made up of a cross-section of people, and everyone thinks differently. For example, the STAR team I am on presently includes a key account manager, two market managers, a category space manager, and a regional general manager. Together, we are formulating better solutions than we would if we were working on the problems individually.

One of the things I've learned is that we cannot always solve the problem, but we can come up with recommendations to make the situation better. Also, many times we need to call people in from specific departments to provide more information on the subject. When we have finalized our recommendations, we present them to the vice president of sales. Sometimes our suggestion is to form a PIT to dive deeper into the subject. At other times, we proposed a solution and ask for approval and a go-ahead.

We have all gone through PIT training, which has changed the way we approach problem solving. Now, whenever a issue comes up, no one says, "What do you think?" We say, "Let's put a PIT together." It has become innate.

At my previous company, I was on a management team that was having problems for a short period of time. A couple of people on the team just didn't care. In the end, those people didn't make it; new people were brought in; the team was able to work well together; and we made things happen. Everyone on a team *has to care.* You can't have two people putting forth all the effort while the others don't participate. It just doesn't work.

The first time you are on a team you think you have all the answers. But once you start talking to the other people you often realize there are more pieces to the puzzle—information you don't have, different perspectives, how it may affect another department, or its impact on costs. The whole team process has been a great learning experience for me.

What I've gained from working with teams is a broader perspective and a sense of accomplishment. Being actively involved in the team process has been rewarding because we are almost always able to come up with a result. At times, that result isn't the final solution to the problem but a step in the right direction. Other times it is and actually helps to improve a situation. Being a part of a team and seeing those results is very satisfying to me.

* * *

If you get the feeling that you can't turn around without bumping into a team or being asked to join one, you are probably right. Teams are ubiquitous in business today; and, since you will probably be on many in your career, it makes sense to be prepared. Years ago, little boys received invaluable team training in sandlots and little league, on the soccer fields, and at the ice rinks. Little girls were at a distinct disadvantage because they didn't play many team sports, but that has changed dramatically. Girls of all ages are playing every conceivable competitive team sport these days; and, when they grow up, they are taking their places beside men as savvy members of productive business teams.

Teams and teamwork are highly valued, as evidenced by their sheer numbers, as well as their breadth of functions. If you are a manager or supervisor, you may spend up to half your time in team-related activities and meetings. But, even if you're not, chances are you are on one or more teams: as a member of a department or a work-group, as half of a joint project, as part of a task force or committee, or as a member of a self-managing work team. Some of these come together for a short period of time and then disband; others stay together longer.

What Is Teamwork?

It takes only two people to make a team, though many teams are much larger. As long as you and one other person are working together toward a common goal, you are part of a team, and you are engaged in the process of teamwork. Teamwork is an orderly, coordinated effort by a group of people who are working together toward a common goal. It is *not* what happens when two or more people have a meeting—formal or informal—to discuss business issues, nor is it just getting along, having fun, or even coming to agreement on a topic.

Teamwork doesn't just miraculously occur whenever a few like-minded folks get together. It must have some essential components in order to work. Though it may comprise several individuals, when these individuals are working together, the team takes on a life of its own. It becomes a single entity, a distinct unit. Its members interact, collaborate, and depend on one another to move them toward their shared goal. While each person may have an individual agenda or objectives, what matters most, and what binds the team together, is its common purpose.

Types of Teams

Teams come in almost as many varieties as people do, but they are a bit easier to classify. Generally speaking, there are two main categories. In the first, the person with power is the team leader; and those who report to that person are team members. In the second, no single person has power; and team members are peers who share equal status.

In a team where the boss is the team leader, the group will almost always acquiesce to that person's desires and take on his or her style. If you are in such a group, and your boss acts like a frustrated Army colonel, you are likely to toe the line and do what you're told. While that is not the most effective environment for promoting team interaction, it is a fairly common scenario. It is not surprising that teams with dysfunctional leaders are usually dysfunctional as well.

On the other hand, peer teams can also run into trouble. They can be inefficient and stumble through meetings, simply because they have no strong leader. They can talk topics to death with no one to keep discussions moving. They may have trouble reaching consensus or following through on decisions. Team members often cave in to peer pressure and just go along with the crowd. While not taking on the leader's style, peer teams do develop a style of their own—a kind of team personality.

One such personality could best be described as a *friendship circle.* Everyone gets along. Nobody rocks the boat or disturbs the illusion of cooperation. In fact, cooperation is the team's guiding principle. Team members enjoy their meetings and each other but don't always accomplish what they set out to do. That's because they don't dig too deeply into tough topics or openly disagree.

Another don't-rock-the-boat style, but a less pleasant one, operates at arm's length from all potentially difficult issues. It's motto might well be *Do nothing, say less, and don't get involved.* Everyone goes through the motions; but, in fact, what matters is doing things right rather than doing the right things. Confronting tough issues is out of the question, and creativity just doesn't happen. It may be the most difficult team on which to get anything accomplished.

Much more dynamic is the type of team that prides itself on tackling the toughest issues, even if that means beating them to death. This team does get things done but often at the expense of its own members. The individual does not become part of the whole but attempts to shine, creating an atmosphere that is more competitive than collaborative. With its *take-no-prisoners* approach, this team is characterized by arguments, verbal jousting, and the not-so-nice games people play at meetings.

Of course, the team everyone wants to be part of is the kind that accomplishes its objectives in creative, synergistic, and productive ways. This ideal team is genuinely collaborative and *in it for the common good,* as opposed to individual glory. Team members seek the best possible solutions and answers and are not afraid to dig around in controversial subjects. Yet, they still manage to remain aware of their collective purpose and each other's needs. Such a team isn't perfect, of course, because it is made up of imperfect people; but it *is* focused and effective. Its secret of success is that all of its members are *team players.*

What Is a Team Player?

There may be no higher praise than to be dubbed *a team player.* In a study conducted by an international outplacement firm, 80 percent of surveyed managers ranked "being a team player" as one of the top three traits they value in their employees. There are ten competencies required to be a team player, according to Andrew J. DuBrin, author of *The Breakthrough Team Player.* Starting with the most basic and building to the more complex, DuBrin breaks these competencies down as follows. A consummate team player:

- Attends team meetings regularly.
- Participates in team brainstorming.
- Works effectively as a team member by:
  - sharing information

- negotiating
- facilitating
- participating
- cooperating
- trusting
- working toward and accepting consensus
- functioning as teacher and learner
- valuing and using leadership skills
- using conflict-resolution skills

- Makes original contributions to team issues and builds upon others' contributions.
- Volunteers to handle action items or to participate in new teams.
- Actively participates in establishing the team's purpose, direction, strategy, or goals.
- Positively questions and challenges others; utilizes conflicting views in a constructive manner.
- Acts to create and promote team cohesiveness.
- Offers to relieve a team member's heavy workload.
- Considers the impact on external interfaces when influencing team outcomes.

Those are the things consummate team players are expected to *do.* Together they compose a lofty goal for anyone. Such behaviors don't all come naturally, but the good news is that they can be learned. What is not so easy to get in a classroom or training class are less tangible characteristics, accompanied by behaviors that reflect their presence. Two indispensable characteristics of a successful team player are self-empowerment and self-discipline.

Empowerment and *self-empowerment,* while they are two sides of the same coin, are not identical. The difference between them is subtle. *Empowerment* is something management bestows upon employees. The word, itself, means to authorize or to enable; to let employees do whatever it takes to get the job done; to tap into the talent, creativity, and problem-solving ability of the work force.

Self-empowerment, on the other hand, begins with the assumption that power is something you already have. To be self-empowered means to use your own power to make your job more satisfying, growth-promoting, and rewarding. It means assuming ownership of and taking responsibility for getting the job done. That's an important characteristic of any team member.

Once you accept your own power and responsibility for your job or role on a team, the second indispensable trait is self-discipline, which DuBrin defines as "mobilizing one's energy and effort to stay focused on attaining an important goal. The outstanding team player pays unswerving attention to team goals and the tasks he or she must accomplish to achieve those goals."

Becoming a Consummate Team Player

No matter how much "comes naturally," it's safe to say that the rest has to be learned. In a business environment where teamwork is highly valued, learning the rules of this game is well worth the effort. Just understanding what it takes and then how to acquire what it takes are two important first steps. Step three, of course, is developing and honing these competencies. Like muscles, they don't just appear as if by magic; they must be strengthened through exercise. "What it takes" to become an effective team player are two sets of competencies: those that apply to tasks and those that refer to people.

Task-related competencies are the *what* of teamwork. They include: sharing special knowledge, taking on tasks and assuming accountability, putting team goals ahead of your own, developing a global view, committing to consensus, tackling tough issues, lending a hand, exchanging favors, and remaining open to new ideas.

- *Sharing special knowledge* assumes that you have some expertise or background on the team's overall purpose or on the subject under discussion. You don't have to be an expert on all aspects of the topic, but you should have something to bring to the party. Otherwise, there is really no reason for you to be there. If the subject is improving productivity in your department, and you have first-hand experience with a computer program that has simplified many of your tasks, that is valuable technical expertise you can share with the group.

Sharing special knowledge or information is as important as having it. While it is true that knowledge is power, this is not the kind of power you keep to yourself. Team players are collaborative, not competitive. You should not only be willing to share what you know, you should have the ability to communicate it so that others will understand the information. For one thing, you can't expect others to take what you say on faith with no explanation. For another, you are being a very poor team player if you withhold information that other people need.

- *Taking on tasks and assuming accountability* means that when some issue or problem is floating around in search of a solution, you will volunteer to seek that solution and you will accept full responsibility for seeing it through. "The five magic words, *It will be my responsibility*, are golden to the team leader and other team members," observes DuBrin. "They now know that this important chunk of the work will be done." Implicit in taking responsibility for doing something is that you can be depended upon to do it. You will produce because you said you would. People count on you, and you come through every time.

- *Putting team goals ahead of your own* acknowledges that you have personal goals that may not always mesh perfectly with your team's goals. As Leslie observed, you aren't on a team to be a star or to pursue your own ends. You are there to work as a group to meet the team's shared objectives. By definition, that means your personal objectives may not be met at this moment. In a cross-functional team there is even more likelihood of a gap between team goals and individual goals. When people from different areas come together to achieve a multidisciplinary purpose, such as improving organizational effectiveness or developing a new product, each person on the team must put the greater good ahead of his or her personal agenda.

   • *Developing a global view* means being able to see the big picture. This is closely linked to staying focused on team goals. It is so easy to put your needs first, to go off on some fascinating tangent, or to get enmeshed in a morass of details and lose sight of the team's mission. Usually it is the team leader's job to remind everyone of the overriding purpose and get the meeting back on track. But sometimes a team member can accomplish the same ends by simply calling attention to the fact that the group discussion has veered off in a nonproductive direction. Either way, someone has to be able to step back and see the process through a wide-angle lens instead of a microscope.

   • *Committing to consensus* means that when the team reaches a decision, everyone on the team supports that decision and takes part in its implementation. You may not like the decision; you may have argued long and hard against it; but once that motion is passed or a conclusion reached, you step back into your role as team player.

   Explains DuBrin, "Believing that consensus is a workable philosophy enables you to participate fully in team decisions without thinking that you have sacrificed your beliefs or the right to think independently." It is not caving in to go along; it is what members of team must do when the debate has ended and the dust has settled. You argue as an individual, but you execute as a team.

A perfect example of committing to consensus is the election process. Candidates express totally polarized views and often say some pretty terrible things about each other. Yet, when the vote it taken, the loser concedes with dignity and throws his or her support behind the winner. At least that's the way it's supposed to be, and the losing candidate risks losing face by appearing to be a spoil sport.

• *Tackling tough issues* means challenging the group's thinking when you must. That's not as easy as it may sound. When everyone is marching off in one direction and you start going in the other direction, it can stir up a lot of emotion. People may get angry; they may not like you; they may run right over you and simply vote their way.

It takes courage to stand up for your point of view and to ask the hard questions no one else is willing to ask. The opposite of this approach is called *Groupthink,* a term coined by Irving L. Janis some years ago to describe the way members of a group become so enmeshed in achieving cohesiveness and camaraderie that they will do anything to avoid dispute, criticism, and making waves.

Asking tough questions helps the group develop insight into the nature of whatever it is grappling with, what it might be doing wrong, or whether it is really getting anywhere. Tough questions can also help a team see the big picture when its mired in minutia.

• *Lending a hand* means helping your fellow team members do a better job of whatever they are doing and pitching in when the work load expands during peak periods. This may not even be team related. When you see a coworker struggling, and you know you can help her improve the way she is doing the job, take some of the load off her shoulders; or simply make constructive suggestions, if it feels appropriate, do it. Try to pick areas where you can really be of use. Offer your strengths when they're needed or just your hands when it's a manual job like collating pages of a report.

Whenever possible, if a coworker or fellow team member makes a request, try to fulfill it. If you turn down enough requests, the other person will stop making them. If you want to be left alone, that's a good way to assure solitude. If, on the other hand you want to be seen as a team player, accept any reasonable request. If you absolutely have to refuse, do so diplomatically. Remember that *how* you do something is sometimes more important than *what* you do or don't do.

• *Exchanging favors* is something good team players do routinely. You make a request, and a coworker says, *Sure, I'd be glad to do that.* Later, he may ask you for a favor; and, if you can, you graciously agree to do it. A spirit of teamwork develops as you engage in these mutually beneficial exchanges. They can be used to facilitate meeting team goals or to build relationships within the group. Here are some examples of exchanges or favors that can foster teamwork:

- You agree to handle a disgruntled caller because one of your coworkers is too stressed out to talk to one more crabby person.

- You cover for a team member who needs a few hours off to take her child to the doctor.

- You agree to attend a soccer game of a friend's son because he can't make it, and his child will be crushed if no one comes to see him play.

- You help a team member put together an important report, knowing she is completely swamped and will never make the deadline.

• *Remaining open to new ideas* means keeping an open mind, a curious outlook, and a willingness to postpone judgment until all sides have been heard from. It means thinking creatively and learning to brainstorm. It means listening carefully and considering other people's views even if they conflict with yours. This is particularly important if you are on a multi-disciplinary team or in a diverse work environment, where people from different backgrounds and areas of specialization bring different ideas to the table.

If work-related competencies are the *what,* those related to people are the *how* of team work. They have everything to do with your interactions with others on your team. Their emphasis is on working with and through people to accomplish shared goals. Consummate team players know that good interpersonal relationships smooth the way for getting things done but are also valuable in their own right. People-related competencies include: trusting team members, sharing the spotlight, acknowledging others' achievements, cooperating and collaborating, listening and sharing information, conveying and accepting constructive criticism, granting the benefit of the doubt, being a team player at the worst of times, and engaging in mutually beneficial exchanges.

• *Trusting team members* is the only way to be on a team. If you don't trust them or believe that they have your best interests at heart, you will be reluctant to share your opinions and suggestions. You will fear the consequences of being too open and vulnerable. As a result, you will hold back. But trusting team members has other implications as well. It means that you believe their ideas and opinions are technically sound and rational, that you are willing to try out their unproven ideas, and that you will risk sharing yours without fear of being ridiculed. Trust takes time to build and yet can be shattered in an instant. Some people will not trust you until you prove you are trustworthy; others will trust you only as long as you are worthy of it. The minute you break it in any way, they will withdraw it permanently.

• *Sharing the spotlight* means you are not in this alone and, if you succeed at something, you probably had a lot of help from your teammates. If you do achieve something noteworthy and receive praise, share it. Without blending into the woodwork, remember that the team takes precedence over the individual. Think *we,* not *I.*

• *Acknowledging others' needs and achievements* means you let them know that you recognize and respect their interests and individual positions. While the team should take precedence, people don't bury their own needs when they become a member. That is as it should be. If you make a suggestion at a meeting, determine if implementing it would create problems for anyone else on the team. If you offer ideas or suggestions, ask if they fit with existing plans or agendas.

Acknowledging achievements is easier to do. For one thing, achievements are usually more obvious; and you don't have dig for them. When a teammate has a significant achievement, compliment him or her. Don't just say something generic like, *You did a good job* or *Way to go!* Make the compliment relevant to what the person has done.

Be sincere and, if you can't, rethink whether and how you might convey your congratulations. What's getting in your way? Is it valid? Are you jealous? If you are going to be a team player, you don't have to love everyone on the team; but you should feel some sense of respect and be genuinely pleased about their accomplishments.

• *Cooperating and collaborating* is the definition of teamwork. Collaboration in the context of teamwork means working with others to solve mutual problems, to achieve shared goals, or to accomplish a task. Working with someone often seems to take longer than going solo, but what you lose in time you will make up in creativity and synergistic effort. Synergy is often explained as 2 + 2 = 5 or 7 or even more. The result of team effort is always greater than the sum of its parts.

Cooperation requires a willingness to work with others for the common good and to get your ego out of the process. For independent, self-sufficient people this is not always easy. But for the sake of the team it's necessary. Also keep in mind that you don't have to pastel out while you're doing this. You are still you, and outside the team process you can be as vivid and as individualistic as you've ever been. Building a cooperative atmosphere sometimes means that you must be the one to make the first move. If you don't observe teamwork going on, take the reins and be the one to initiate it.

• *Listening and sharing* means using what is known as "active listening," being truly engaged in trying to understand the meaning and emotions behind the words. That requires paying attention to not only the words but to the nonverbal cues, body language, and invisible signals you take in through your sixth sense. Active listening means checking for understanding and reflecting back the feelings you are getting. A teammate may say, *OK, I buy that. I'll go along with the plan;* but if you sense reluctance, don't accept the words. Trust your intuitive reading of the real message, and probe a bit deeper.

Listening is the taking-in side of communication; sharing is the sending-out side. You must be willing to share what you know, and you must develop the communication skills to do so effectively. The team needs your information in whatever form it comes, which can range from a formal presentation to a report to a rumor you hear through the grapevine that should be checked out for accuracy.

• *Conveying and accepting constructive criticism* puts emphasis on the word *constructive.* When you feel criticism is needed and you're the one to offer it, remember that delivery counts. If you must criticize, do it in a way that will not hurt the other person's feelings. Keep it to a minimum, and don't deliver a dissertation. Focus on the other person's work or suggestion, *not* on the person. Keep it in passive form, as in *The plan is pretty good, but it could be better organized,* as opposed to *You didn't organize it correctly.* This is a small but powerful difference. You might also ask a question to buffer the point, such as *Do you think it might be organized a little differently to make it flow more smoothly?*

Hard as it is to dispense criticism, it's even harder to accept it. Yet it is often necessary. If the criticism is offered in the right spirit and you are able to see it as feedback meant to help you improve, you will reap many benefits. Statements like, *Don't take it personally* or *Don't be so defensive* may be good advice but are almost as tough to take as the criticism. Constructive criticism provides an opening for self-evaluation. Ask yourself, *Is it warranted? Is it accurate? Is it well intentioned? Should I change something in the way I'm operating?* One last point: Thank the person who delivers it. It will enhance your stature a hundredfold.

• *Granting the benefit of the doubt* means not rushing to judgment. Stay flexible. Be willing to believe and accept what someone says rather than debating it into the ground. If you sincerely doubt its veracity, ask a few questions; but then acquiesce, at least once. If you find time after time that you are having trouble buying in to the same person's information, then it will be time to examine the facts.

• *Being a team player at the worst of times* means, once again, that the team's needs often supersede your own. Doing what is best for the team may inconvenience you or take up time you feel you can't spare, but your reputation as a team player is at stake here. If you can delegate work or find people to pitch in and help, that will help. But then you have asked a favor, and will technically owe a favor. That's what engaging in mutually beneficial exchanges is all about: *You help me; I'll help you.* It is also what being a team player is all about.

Conclusion

There is a delicate balance between making a name for yourself as a high achiever and keeping out of the spotlight as a member of a team. It is much the same as going back and forth between being a soloist and blending your voice with a chorus. There is a time and a place for both. The same spirit of enthusiasm and commitment you bring to individual pursuits is necessary for being a consummate team player. Every member of a team should be a dynamic, involved, hard-working person. You won't leave all of that outside the door when you enter a meeting. You will simply focus your energy on what this group has come together to do. It takes strong individuals to be consummate team players.

CHAPTER FOUR

Learning to Negotiate

Gregg Ganschaw is CEO of I to I Consulting, a firm that works with organizations of all types to initiate or cope with change. As a hands-on facilitator, he has conducted hundreds of programs on change and negotiation and witnessed what he describes as nothing short of miraculous outcomes. Mr. Ganschaw's background with the National Security Agency (NSA), several major corporations, and the national speakers' circuit make him not only an expert but a very compelling seminar leader.

Negotiation is the combined effort of individuals to reach an agreement that the majority feels is in its best interest. As the CEO of a company primarily involved in facilitating organizational change, negotiations make up the sum total of everything I do with groups. Whether these groups are teenagers in youth-at-risk programs, chief executive officers, owners of companies, supervisors, or hourly employees, I negotiate 60 minutes per hour while I am facilitating, in order to get the group where it needs to go. What I have been able to observe in that process is that, although every group is different in composition, there are three essential things that *must* take place for negotiation to work.

The first is the initial exchange of information, so that the parties understand where the other side is coming from and why this topic is relevant to them. The second builds on that, creating a sense of identification and trust. The third is that everyone with any influence on the negotiation understands the potential outcome and the available options. These three parts pretty much lay out the playing field. If they are done up front, and if they are done right, then *almost any topic* can be negotiated successfully. If they are *not* done up front, or if they are not done in a positive spirit, there will be a lesser degree of buy in. Less buy in leads to a more protracted, more negative negotiation period.

We are currently working with a regional location of a major corporation, where we have management on one side and the union on the other. They have had an adversarial relationship for thirty to forty years. Often, it is the facilitator's or mediator's job to find a point of agreement that will get everyone to the table. Sometimes it takes days, if not weeks, to find a real common point both sides feel is worth pursuing. That is the first brick in the wall. In this case, both sides have come up with their own common point in wanting to sustain their particular business unit. They see that if they don't come together and find a way to deal with their past difficulties, their future may be very brief.

What we have to do is set up four basic planks for this negotiation to be successful. The first plank is to provide a safe space in which to conduct the negotiation. We have to remove as many of the physical obstacles as possible so that neither side feels it is starting from a diminutive position. The second plank is giving each side an opportunity to vent—to get its story on the table—without causing a greater rift between the two sides. Normally, the venting process takes place separately. A mediator creates a safe environment for each side to get the poison out. Once both sides have exhausted that poison, we bring them together. The third plank is ensuring that both sides feel they are being heard. Each point is laid out and fed back so that both sides have a chance to say, "This is what I heard," or "No, that's not what I said," or "Well that's close. Let me say it a different way." That process takes place back and forth, back and forth, until all of the positions have been put on the table.

Often, the ultimate negotiation will end up taking place between as few as two people, once those responsible for reaching agreement on the goals have done so. We give those two people the outline and the rules, which, again, are a safe space, a belief that each side has been heard, common objectives, and feedback. The feedback loop is important to ensure that, as each agreement is reached, everyone has the same understanding of what it is.

The two things that get through to people are *benefit* and *pain.* We call them "pay value" and "threat." Pain would be when your boss says, "You two need to work out a way to get along and work together in this department, or I am going to fire you both." Pay value could be a promotion or anything considered a perk. The pain or the pay value has to be strong enough to get people beyond their emotional positions.

One of those two most likely brought these groups to the point where they were willing to sit down at the table. If there is a fear of loss, that also gets people's attention. Loss is painful, but the pain has to become significant enough to do something about it. Then, our job is to convert that pain into something of value.

The key to the whole process is finding *one point of common ground* to which both sides can relate. There is a story of a very heated negotiation between two national leaders, and the mediator being unable to find a way to help them see each other as trusted individuals. They had two hundred years of history, animosity, and labels in the room with them. Finally, quite by accident, the mediator came upon a common denominator. Both of these leaders were males and both were married. Both were having similar difficulties with their wives and their married children. When they began to see each other as husbands and fathers with similar problems, they could talk. The mediator used that common ground to melt their antagonism.

It is possible for two people who don't see eye-to-eye on a topic to negotiate without a mediator as long as the pain or pay value is strong enough to get them beyond their emotional positions. For a long-term settlement to work, though, both sides must believe that their mutual needs are being met. If a loss is perceived, the side that perceives it will find a way to consciously or unconsciously sabotage the agreement.

* * *

Life is a series of negotiations, large and small. Because no two people are alike, each of us has different needs and desires. Alone, we can at least try to fill them without interference; with someone else in the picture, it becomes more complicated. From something as inconsequential as which movie to see or restaurant to choose for dinner to such global concerns as the nuclear arms race or peace in the Middle East, ultimately, we must talk it over and come to some mutually acceptable agreement.

That is precisely what negotiation is—the process of discussing a topic with the intention of arriving at an agreement that meets both parties' needs. In negotiating, neither side is supposed to exercise the power of position, even if one person has such power; bulldoze or manipulate; or just cave in to the other person's demands. Presumably, a negotiation is a meeting of equals who come together to work through issues until they reach consensus.

The ability to negotiate is one of the most valuable arrows you can have in your quiver. It will have a tremendous impact on your ability to get what you want, in the business world and in your private life. It will help you meet your needs and get ahead without running roughshod over other people. Negotiating well is not the exclusive province of heads of state, diplomats, CEOs, and attorneys. It is open to the public, so to speak; and we all do it whether we realize it or not. In fact, if you want to see it done well, watch a child.

"Children are excellent negotiators," says Frank L. Acuff, author of *How to Negotiate Anything With Anyone Anywhere in the World.* "They are persistent. They don't know the meaning of the word *no. They* do know that when we say no, we often mean maybe. They are never embarrassed. They often read *us* better than we read *them.*"

Acuff maintains that there are only seven subjects on which we negotiate: price; terms; delivery; quality; service; training; and resources, including people, money, and materials. All others, he insists, are variations on those themes.

"Not counting physical force, intimidation, manipulation, coercion, or extortion, there are only three methods anyone can use to get action from other people," writes Norbert Aubuchon in the *Anatomy of Persuasion. They* are command, persuade, and negotiate. Command is usually a last resort, when one person has the power and nothing else has worked. Persuasion is a primary method of achieving a desired outcome from another person. Like negotiation, persuasion requires interactive communications. Unlike negotiation, its nature is usually nonadversarial; and those who are persuaded, says Aubuchon, almost always feel comfortable and satisfied with the outcome. That, of course, is also the goal of negotiation.

Win/Win: Is It Possible?

Going for a win/win is the much-touted goal of every interaction, but particularly of any interaction aimed at a negotiated settlement. Win/win, in a nutshell, is a desire that any agreement reached will be to the mutual benefit and satisfaction of both sides. Win/win is cooperative, as opposed to competitive or adversarial. Ideally, everyone is pleased with the outcome; and no one feels short-changed.

Of course, there are situations in which a win/win outcome is not desirable. If you are in a competitive situation—a sport or a contest or a race, for example—the idea is for one side to win, and you want it to be your side. Win/win doesn't make much sense in such a scenario. But negotiation is not a contest or a competitive event. It is ultimately a meeting of the minds. Thus, if after discussion, you are persuaded that the other side has a good point, you will probably compromise or agree to his demands. If the relationship with the other person means more to you than winning, you might say that and do it her way.

Then, there are those circumstances where a win/win is the only possibility you will accept. Author and consultant Stephen Covey calls this: "win/win or no deal." *No deal* basically means that if you cannot come to a meeting of the minds on which you can both agree and derive benefit, you close the discussion and walk away. Going for a win/win isn't a strategy. It is an attitude in which you are prepared to speak honestly, listen wholeheartedly, and elicit the other person's needs so that you can address them.

Everyone gives lip service to idea of win/win; and, in fact, most people enter a negotiation really believing that is their objective. In real life, however, no matter how positive one's intentions, when the going gets tough, adversaries often get tougher. Despite your intellectual acceptance of the value of win/win, the game may well deteriorate into I win/you lose. The problem with that is that the loser isn't always a good sport about the outcome and may be planning his or her revenge before the ink dries on the agreement.

"Win/win negotiation is critical," say Frank Acuff, "not for you to be a wonderful, kind human being, but because it is the *practical* thing to do. It will help you get more of what you want in two key ways: by meeting the needs of the other person and by focusing on *interests,* rather than on *positions* … Positions are almost always unresolvable, but uncovering interests helps you access the real needs of the other person."

"Accessing the real needs of the other person" is the cornerstone of effective negotiations. Even if that person doesn't believe you are honorable in your intentions and fair in your methods, or if the conditions under which you are negotiating are not conducive to collaboration and trust, if you sincerely attempt to discover what your counterpart needs and make a genuine attempt to provide it, barriers will begin to crumble, no matter what the circumstances.

Stages of Negotiations

The negotiation process is, by its very nature, somewhat structured. If it is to be effective, it must follow some logical framework. That framework, according to Acuff, has six very distinct stages: orientation and fact finding, resistance, reformulation of strategies, hard bargaining and decision making, agreement, and follow-up.

1. *Orientation and Fact Finding* come first because they are the foundation upon which you will build your negotiating strategy. If you don't yet believe that knowledge is power, this is the proving ground for that statement. It's important to gather the information you will need up front, before you ever sit across the table (the traditional forum for negotiation) from the other person. How familiar are you with your counterpart? What do you know about her desires and present position in regard to these talks? Is this the first such conversation or is this routine operating procedure for this person? What is her style in such a situation? Who has the authority here—you or she? What do you hope to get out of this? What does she? What are the consequences of failing to reach a mutual agreement?

2. *Resistance* is a fact of life in such discussions. Negotiations are not tea parties; and, no matter how skillful you are, they can be very difficult. In fact, if there isn't any resistance, you should worry because it could mean that the other person is just going through the motions and couldn't care less. The upside of resistance is that it can help you gather more information about where that person is coming from and what is bothering her. If you don't know what her objections are you can't ever hope to overcome them. The basic questions you need answered if you are to break through resistance are: *What is causing this? What is she objecting to? What's in it for her to participate and cooperate?*

Perhaps she is testing your limits, pushing to see how far you are willing to go and where you will draw the line. She may be an analytical sort of person whose objections are completely logical. This is one of the easier sources of resistance with which to deal. On the other hand, she may be acting out of pure emotion, finding either you, the subject of the discussion, or this whole process distasteful and stressful. This is one of the tougher ones because you will have to encourage her to vent, listen and observe to find out what the problem is; and put her at ease before you can proceed.

Maybe she is averse to change and leaving her comfort zone, and that's just what you are proposing. Or maybe she just cannot do what you wish because of company policy, her boss's stand on this issue, or any one of a number of reasons that are completely outside her sphere of influence. Finally, her reason may be as simple as a determination *not* to make any concessions at your first meeting. Whatever the reason, this is a hurdle you must overcome before you get to stage three, or there won't be a stage three.

3. *Reformulation of Strategies* occurs when you gather new information that renders your plan obsolete or at least slightly off kilter. No matter how great your strategies seemed, it is foolhardy to stick with them if they no longer apply. As you are getting a handle on how much the other person wants to reach an agreement, what her particular negotiating style is, and how things are progressing, it is wise to reassess your approach and change it if necessary.

4. *Hard Bargaining and Decision Making* mean it is time to get serious. This is the part of the process where you dig in to determine the other person's real objectives, not just her stated ones. *What is standing in the way? How can you overcome those hurdles? What are the key issues here? What is in it for you and for her to reach agreement?* Be creative in framing your proposed solutions.

5. *Agreement* means not only shaking hands on the broad framework but also hammering out the details of the deal. It also means being absolutely certain you

both understand that to which you have agreed. If you need someone else's signature on this agreement, get it. If you are the only one who must say *yea* or *nay,* wrap it up.

6. *Followup* is one of the most important and least applied stages of the negotiation process, which should not end with a signature or a handshake. If you do this step correctly, you are setting the stage for the next negotiation, should there be a need for one.

Nuts and Bolts

While understanding the stages of negotiation is important, it provides only the broad framework of how to engage effectively in this process. Negotiations may vary by industry; by purpose; by issues; by circumstances; and, as the world becomes a global economy, certainly by country and culture. Therefore, generalizing about how to do it is not a good idea. On the other hand, there are some principles that apply to all negotiating situations. They are planning your negotiation strategies, having high aspirations, thinking win/win and meaning it, getting your message across in understandable English, having a spirit of inquiry, establishing genuine relationships, maintaining your integrity, not giving away the store, and hanging in there for as long as the process requires.

Plot Your Course

Walking into a negotiation without planning in advance is like throwing the fight before you step in the ring. Thorough preparation is a critical first step and not a terribly complicated one. It begins with identifying *all* of the issues that may come up on either side. Don't be content with a superficial, off-the-top-of-your-head list. Brainstorm with others, sleep on it, add things as they pop into your mind, let your creativity rip, and draft a very long list of every possible issue that could surface in the discussion.

After you have your list, put the issues in order of importance. Do this with your issues and with those you believe to be the other person's issues. You will probably be more accurate about yours than his, but this is a good way to start thinking in terms of what the other person wants.

Look over your prioritized lists, and see if you can find areas in which agreement *might* be reached. Then answer these questions: *What is the agreement you would want in the best of all possible worlds? Since it isn't the best of all possible worlds, what do you really want? If you don't get it, what will you settle for? What is your bottom line? And, finally, what would it take to kill the deal?* Then repeat this entire process as you imagine how the other person would answer the same questions. Put yourself in his shoes, and think as he would think.

The next step is to develop strategies and tactics that will get you from where you are to where you want to go and, at the same time, meet the needs of the other person. Strategies are big picture approaches to an issue; tactics are the specific actions you will take to implement your strategy. Tactics are the *how* part of achieving your ends. According to Frank Acuff, "Tactics may include whether or not to make the first offer, how much to offer, when to make concessions, and the speed at which you plan to make concessions."

What separates skilled negotiators from less skillful ones are actions such as these, done during the planning processes:

- Skilled negotiators consider twice as many action possibilities and potential outcomes.
- They spend more than three times as much effort on trying to find common ground.

- They devote more than twice the time on long-term issues.
- They maintain flexibility by setting specific objectives within a range, rather than finite, one-point objectives.
- They discuss each issue on its own merits, rather than lumping them together or going through them in a predetermined order.

Go for a Win/Win ... In Earnest

You already understand how important a win/win attitude is. Your challenge now is to convert that attitude into action. The first step is to tune into WIIFM—What's In It For Me? That is surely what the other person is asking. *Why do this? How will I benefit?* Win/win means both of you have to be able to satisfactorily answer WIIFM. Your job is to anticipate the other person's response.

What makes that difficult is that often two people appear to be going in the same direction when, in fact, they are not. That happens when you don't bother to verify your understanding of the other person's real objectives on the front end. If you don't know what they are, you can't possibly meet them. You will also find yourself eating up precious time and energy fighting your way through this negotiation only to discover that you and the other person are working at cross-purposes.

Another aspect of win/win is how much time you spend on defensive behaviors, offensive behaviors, and disagreements. Odd as it may seem, skilled negotiators tend to spend *less* time on all three than one might think. They also don't amass a pile of arguments to support their positions because they know that a few strong arguments will be more effective than a bushel basket full of distracting, smaller ones.

Whatever actions you adopt, remember that your underlying attitude must be one of genuine desire for the other person's needs, as well as your own, to be met and for both of you to feel positive about the outcome.

Aim High

Going into negotiations, your aspirations should be high, even lofty. Why *not* reach for the sky? Remember that you have already thought through your expectations before you sit down at the table. You know what you are asking for, what you really want, and at what point you will go no further.

There are sound reasons for asking for a lot on the front end. For one thing, if you go in low, you are undercutting your own power. The other person may do that to you, but you don't want to do it to yourself. For another, going in high sends a clear message about how you expect to be treated. It also lowers the other person's expectations. Finally, going in high demonstrates your seriousness and staying power.

Going in high will require more time, but in that time you can learn a great deal about the other person. Since what you are asking for is not what you really want or what you will settle for, the bargaining process will allow your opponent to think he is wearing you down and feel some sense of victory. That is more important than you may realize.

Communicate Clearly

The single most important element in any negotiation is communication, which encompasses a host of subtopics. These include how well you listen, how clearly and concisely you get your point across, how well you interpret nonverbal cues, and whether you say what you mean or dance around the point. Here are a few basic guidelines to keep in mind:

• If you are dealing with someone from another country—which could certainly be the case, as more and more American companies do business abroad or are bought by foreign enterprises—do not assume that, because your counterpart says she speaks English, she fully understands it or can carry on a conversation.

• Avoid jargon and business-ese, which is a kind of an elitist shorthand for real communication. For example, expressions like annual *premium,* when you mean *payment,* or *accrued* interest when you could say *unpaid,* or *maturity date,* when that is merely when the final payment is due, come under the heading of unnecessary jargon.

• Simplify English words, terms, and colloquialisms, whether you are talking to someone from another country, another region of your own country, or another company down the street. What is clearly understood in the U.S. may not be in China. Closer to home, pet phrases from Cincinnati or Tallahassee may not be part of the lingo in San Francisco or New York. Some words that could be easily simplified include, *commence* (start); *acquaint you with* (tell you); *endeavor* (try); and *modification* (change). Good writers go for the simple and straightforward; good speakers, in any situation, should do so as well.

• Minimize slang and sports metaphors, especially if the person with whom you are negotiating is not familiar with the sport. *Have we covered all the bases?* may not be interpreted as *Have we considered all of our options? We are not going to throw in the towel* is a boxing expression that means *We're not giving up,* but does everyone know that? Don't assume so.

Ask Questions and Listen Up

If you have mastered the art of questioning, you are at a distinct advantage in any negotiation. In the first stage—orientation and fact finding—what you are after is information, and you don't get information when you do all the talking. Delivering a stirring monologue may be good for your ego, but it is like trying to close a sale before you even know what the customer's needs are.

Consistently effective negotiators ask twice as many questions as less effective ones. Why? Because questions are the most powerful tool you have for reaching out to the other person, accumulating knowledge, understanding both the message and emotions behind it, and verifying what you heard and understood.

- Questions give the other person an opportunity to talk, which he certainly will do.
- Question are more apt to be attended to than are statements.
- Questions help clarify fuzzy thinking—yours and the other person's.
- Questions organize the problem and help you find a solution.
- Questions defuse a volatile situation by getting the facts out on the table and giving everyone involved a chance to vent their emotions.
- Questions keep the discussion focused on a solution or a decision.
- Questions help people evaluate possible options.
- Questions surface and address objections.
- Questions certainly open the lines of communication between people in a negotiation.

In reality, there are only two types of questions—open and closed. You ask a *closed question* when you're looking for a piece of information, confirmation of a fact, someone's attention, or closure in the conversation. Closed questions are answered with yes or no, a few words, or a sentence or two. They are very targeted and brief. They don't encourage a dissertation or a great deal of discussion.

Open questions, on the other hand, do encourage exploration and more questions. You ask an open question when you want information, opinions, observations, and feelings. Open questions allow the other person to become involved, to participate in the exchange, to think about their answers, and to come up with solutions of their own. With open questions, you gain far more than factual information. You also get a good handle on the thoughts, attitudes, and emotions that influence the other person's actions.

Build Genuine Relationships

You may already have a relationship with the other person that you would like to preserve, or this might be an opportunity to establish one. Obviously, you don't want to torpedo any relationship, whether it already exists or is in its embryonic stages. With that in mind, it's a good idea to avoid topics that involve values, such as politics, religion, race, and the role of women in the workplace. They are rarely neutral. In fact, they tend to inflame.

You want a to make a connection with this person, even if it only lasts through the meeting. In many countries, the quality of the relationship is more important than the work being done or the outcome of the negotiations. In this country, that is not usually so, but perhaps it should be. Trust is not established unless a relationship of some kind exists, so it only makes good sense to be sure it does.

What you say and how you say it in this meeting of the minds will affect any future negotiations you may have with this person. This is true even if you don't bring this discussion to a satisfactory close. Sometimes what you're really doing is setting the stage for next time, rather than trying to "win" this one this time.

Be True to Yourself

It cannot be news that personal integrity is the basis for all relationships, but none more so than this one. There are two reasons why integrity and trust are vital, writes Frank Acuff. "The first reason has to do with information. No one tells you anything of importance if he or she doesn't trust you ... The second reason [is that] issues of trust are the most difficult relationship problems to repair. In fact, these are often irreparable ... The trust issue hardly ever gets fixed."

Building trust can take a long time and, despite your best efforts, can easily and inexplicably be derailed. How do *you* feel when someone says to you, *To be honest with you* ... or *To tell the truth* ... or *Frankly* ...? Are you not usually honest, truthful, and candid? The other person may not even know why she doesn't trust you, but chances are good the reason is one of those trust-buster phrases or something similar.

If you are trusted, do nothing to jeopardize that status. Says Acuff, "Lose the deal if you must, but keep the trust."

Conserve Concessions

Concessions reveal a great deal about you to your negotiating partner. How you use them sets a tone and tells him how to treat you now and in any future negotiations. Concessions can be tricky and can backfire. On the other hand, they can accomplish exactly what you had in mind if you:

- Are not the first to make a concession on an issue of importance.
- Don't accept the first offer.
- Make the other person come down on his first demand.
- Don't honor that first demand by making a counteroffer.
- Make small concessions to lower the other person's expectations.

- Make concessions that are important to the other person but unimportant to you.
- Defer conceding on issues that matter to you.
- Make your concessions contingent on getting something in return.
- Celebrate what you gain, and don't feel guilty.
- Refrain from meeting every concession on the other person's part with one of your own.

Patience, Patience, Patience

Patience is more than a virtue; it is a necessity in negotiations. Patience achieves three things: It helps you get the information you need; it builds the relationship you want; and it increases your effectiveness. Of course, you aren't the only one at the table who knows the value of patience. The other person may be using the same tactic. Her goal in that case is to wear you down and wear you out. Don't let that happen. Here is how to remain patient in the face of such a strategy:

- Give yourself all the time you need.
- Relax and get comfortable.
- Be aware, and tell anyone else who should know, that this process may take quite a while.
- Believe that this whole thing may be harder for the other person than it is for you.
- Think about establishing a deadline for ending the talks.

Patience is hard work, but it's worth it. It is only time, after all; and, while time supposedly is money, it is also on your side. If you want a positive, win/win outcome, you must invest yourself, your energy, and whatever time is required.

Conclusion

In any negotiation, the other person will see things your way because he feels good when he does or because doing so solves a problem for him. There are also logical and emotional aspects to consider. To successfully conclude negotiations, you must satisfy both the logical and emotional needs of the other person and convince him that this is your final offer, your bottom line.

Most negotiators, particularly Americans dealing with people from other countries, tend to stress logic, research, and hard facts. When you're negotiating with someone who thinks on the left side of his brain, this can be very convincing. But no matter whom you are dealing with, don't ignore the emotional side of the equation. Emotions often play a bigger part in decisions than logic. If the other person's emotional needs are not met, it can totally block his ability or desire to ever look at the facts you have so painstakingly assembled.

Finally, you have to convince the other person that you have gone as far as you will go. If you have established a relationship built on trust, he will believe you; and you will enter the final phase of your discussion—hammering out the final agreement.

CHAPTER FIVE

Building Trust

Timothy McKenna is vice-president of Investor Relations & Communications for Jefferson Smurfit Corporation, a publicly traded paper and packaging company. His audiences range from Wall Street financial analysts and individual shareholders to 16,000 employees and the national business press. His credibility is on the line every time he answers a question from the media, sends out a press release, or signs off on a newsletter or the annual report.

Trust is the heart of what I do as a professional—on the communication side, but even more so on the investor relations side. For most of my career in corporate communications, I've been involved in media relations or investor relations, which means I've been in the role of a spokesman. The only thing I have going for me is *trust*. I can't hope to influence the money managers I work with unless they know they can trust me. I never lie to them. If things are bad, I tell them they're bad; and if they're good, I tell them they're good. It's been the heart of what I do, and it is also the way I conduct all of my business dealings.

I may approach this issue a little differently from others I know. I don't view communicating with an external or internal audience, with my peers or my subordinates, with Wall Street or the press as really any different. What it comes down to is that I must *always* tell the truth. There are some situations where I am less constrained. There are others where the confidentiality of the information doesn't permit me to tell people what they want to know. Under any circumstances, I never mislead anyone or tell them a lie. To me, honesty doesn't mean just saying things that are not false. It means observing the *spirit* of truth, not just the letter of truth.

Most of the people I work closely with trust me because they know that if they ask me something or tell me something, they'll get a consistent response. Certainly, they know that if they ask me to do something, I'll do it; or I'll tell them I can't do it. So they can depend on me. They also know that if they make a mistake or unintentionally reveal something about themselves, I'm not going to use it against them.

You can't have any kind of open relationship with people unless you are willing to reveal your weaknesses. And, if you are open, inevitably you *will* reveal your weaknesses, as well as your strengths. You have to have confidence that, when you do, the other person isn't going to use it as ammunition. I'm pretty cautious with people, because I have found the business world to be a pretty cold place. On the other hand, I have learned to trust my instincts. My way of doing things is to trust people little by little, see what happens over time, and try to build on that.

Everybody has a certain degree of openness, but it is different for each person. Some people are more comfortable revealing their personal quirks and feelings than others. The current president of my company is very open and will let you see who he really is without hesitation. The past president of the company, on the other hand, is a very private person. Yet, both of them are absolutely consistent in their behavior. You can trust them completely.

Some people are very open; others are very cautious. Most people fall somewhere in the middle. They determine what they're comfortable with and develop a trusting relationship over time, based on gut feelings and experience. It would be nice to say that in every environment you're going to find some sort of formula that works and be able to build trust with people. But, in truth, I don't think that's possible.

From my own experience, I've learned that relationships in business *can* be genuine friendships. But, unfortunately, that is rare. I've read people wrong from time to time. I've trusted them and discovered later that we were playing the game by different rules. It wasn't a pleasant discovery.

I've had some conversations with younger people about this subject, and I've cautioned them not to get confused and believe that any relationship they build at work is automatically a genuine friendship. It may not be. Frankly, it is not a good idea to be too open too quickly or to communicate who you are and what you think immediately. You have to hold back at first. I think this is particularly important for those just entering the business world. Young people, coming out of college, can easily find themselves in situations where warmth and openness are misinterpreted.

When it comes to trusting others and being the kind of person others can trust, I don't think there are any simple answers, but here are my basic guidelines: Be true to yourself, but don't be reckless. Let others reveal themselves before you do. Test the waters, and then proceed slowly. And, finally, trust your instincts.

* * *

Trust, according to most dictionaries, means *assured reliance on the character, ability, strength, or truth of someone or something.* To trust is *to have confidence in, to rely on, to believe.*

Trust in this country is becoming an endangered species. On every level, it is being disregarded, abused, and killed. Nationally, justice isn't exactly blind; she is merely selective in what she chooses to see or to ignore. Politically, with every sentence crafted into a sound byte for the six o'clock news and critics undermining every position before it is even taken; with scandals, special investigators, and revelations daily occurrences; and with parties and politicians alike saying one thing on Monday and reversing their story on Tuesday, trust has become a joke. Personally, relationships are built on shifting sands, with both sides afraid of the "C word" (commitment); the divorce rate is staggering; infidelity, abuse, and skipping out on child support are common practices.

In business, cynicism is the order of the day. False claims, outright lies, broken contracts, law suits at the drop of a hat, behind-the-scenes deal making, and employees feeling sold out have killed any semblance of trust that might once have existed. Employees complain of having little or no input into major changes that affect their lives. They know, too, that they can no longer look to their employers for job security. A survey conducted by a Pennsylvania consulting firm found that trust has declined at three out of four workplaces over the past two years and has hit a low point in corporate America.

Could this possibly be a surprise to anyone? The social contract between U.S. companies and employees was broken years ago. In fact, it has been smashed beyond recognition. The headlines relentlessly call our attention to mergers and acquisitions, restructurings and downsizings, and the resulting elimination of thousands of jobs.

We read those headlines, becoming increasingly numb to the numbers, and sometimes forget that it is *people* who once held those jobs. It is *people* who are seeing their plans unravel and their security threatened, often with little or no warning. It is *people* who must carry out the mandate to lay off X number of employees and get a head count down to some minute percentage of what it was. It is *people* who have lost faith in their corporations. But it is also *people* who run those corporations. Trust is a person-to-person issue.

Trust: How to Create It, Cultivate It, Keep It Alive

• *Admit your mistakes.* This is difficult for everyone, especially in a business setting where the stakes seem so high. But when you've erred, others probably know it anyway. So, own up to your mistakes and, even more important, apologize when you are wrong. No one ever died from saying, "I'm sorry," but many relationships have been saved as a result.

• *Be consistent and congruent.* There should be no discrepancy between what you say and what you do. People cannot count on you if you react one way today and another way tomorrow.

• *Be decisive and follow through.* Don't waffle all over the place when a decision has to be made. Just make it; but, when you do, be prepared to do what you said you'd do. Even something as small as saying, "I'll call you," and failing to do so undermines trust.

- *Risk being real.* Honesty begins with being who you are and letting others see that person. It's difficult to put on an act forever, and sooner or later, people will see through a performance. What could be worse than being thought of as "a phony"?

- *Be absolutely honest.* Is anyone *absolutely* honest? Don't we all tell little white lies? Not if you want to be believed. You have to be completely and consistently straight with people. Don't manipulate them. Delivery counts, of course. How you say what you say is as important as saying it.

- *Be true to yourself and your values.* Integrity is the basis of trust. If there is anything that destroys it, it is the feeling that a person is without a solid sense of ethics.

- *Listen with an open mind, and respect others' opinions.* If you have a predetermined conclusion before others speak, you know it and they know it. But if you attempt to understand and be open to what you hear, you might learn something you didn't know. Every opinion is worth hearing, even if you don't agree with it.

- *Focus on shared goals more than on personal agendas.* Ask yourself, What is best for the common good, as opposed to what's in it for me? Try to see the big picture instead of focusing on your private ambitions. When you only care about yourself, it's difficult for others to trust you.

- *Give credit where credit is due.* Don't you know someone who will take ownership of any idea or achievement, even if it rightfully belongs to someone else? If the team as a whole did something great, say so. If you receive a compliment, but it was a coworker who should have it, make that clear. There is plenty of recognition to go around.

- *Honor your commitments, keep your promises, be reliable.* They all mean the same thing. Be there when it counts. If you say you'll do something, do it. If you give your word, keep it.

• *Maintain confidences.* When someone shares something private with you, when you hold proprietary information, when confidentiality is important, *don't* pass it on. It is that simple.

• *Play fair.* It starts on the playground and stays with you all the way through your life. Play by the rules. Don't cheat. Don't stack the deck in your favor or anyone else's. Do the right thing, always. That's the stuff trust is made of.

• *Say what you mean.* It's amazing how many people speak in code. Their words are so convoluted, we often don't know what they said. If you can't be straightforward, don't say anything. If you do speak, be clear, be direct, be honest. Don't obscure your meaning with unnecessary verbiage.

• *Show respect for people at all levels.* Would you trust someone who all but bowed to people in "power" and treated secretaries, store clerks, and all the regular folks of the world with disdain and contempt? Probably not. Enough said?

• *Start from a position of trust.* There are two ways of approaching trust: (1) trusting someone on the front end and withdrawing it if the person proves untrustworthy; or (2) withholding trust until you're sure it's warranted. Risk trying number one.

• *Take responsibility for your own actions.* Don't pass the buck. Don't blame others. Don't remain silent. If you said something, made a decision, or took an action, own up to it. Remember George Washington and the cherry tree? Every child learns that story for good reason.

Building Trust, Breaking Trust

Corporate vision statements are the "in thing" of the nineties. They provide a unifying theme; they build morale; they become the focal point for all kinds of activities and celebrations; and, best-case scenario, they help to move the organization in a new direction. There isn't anything bad about corporate visions. Like Mom and apple pie, they are just what is needed to energize companies, rally the troops, and build trust, *unless* they are mishandled. Then, they become the Terminator, destroying everything in their path, especially trust. Consider three companies who tried to craft a vision and how trust was either established and nurtured or completely and forever ruptured.

Company A was privately owned by two partners who were as different from each other as any two people could be. They agreed on absolutely nothing but, in spite of that, had managed to build a fairly successful business over the years. One of the partners decided the company needed a mission, so he assembled the management committee to create one. When the committee, with much guidance from that partner, arrived at an acceptable concept, the vice president of communications was instructed to "clean it up and give it some punch."

The draft was then disseminated to all employees with a request to comment on anything they liked, disliked, or wanted to add. It was understood that everyone at the management level was expected to respond, which they did. It was predicted that few people below the management level would do so, which they didn't. When the responses came in, they were considered by the management committee. Few were actually incorporated into the final draft.

When the vision was completed, printed, and nicely framed, the company closed down for a day to roll it out at a special ceremony. Some members of the management committee made brief speeches. Employees were asked for their candid comments and questions; but, since this was a company that had never encouraged candor in the past, few people risked saying anything meaningful.

Everyone attended a company-wide luncheon and then reconvened at the office for a series of department meetings, at which employees were to ask real questions and express real feelings in a "safe environment." Since there were very few environments that had ever been considered safe, these meetings were, for the most part, fairly constrained.

What followed was a flurry of activity, as each department created its own mission and strategic objectives, based on the corporate mission. When those were approved, the next step was to come up with concrete action plans. All of this consumed several months of intense effort, while, at the same time, business as usual was being conducted.

At last, the reams of paper generated by the process were approved, and each department set about working their action plans. By this time, there was a lot of enthusiasm for the process. People, down to the most cynical, believed things might actually be changing, though they had never thought it possible. Some worried that the partners wouldn't have the staying power to see this through, but they were careful to keep such thoughts to themselves.

In the midst of all this bustling activity and guarded hope, the sales figures for two quarters in a row plummeted. The partners agreed on one thing: That was unacceptable. There were many meetings behind closed doors and solemn faces in the halls. Pressure was applied; people buckled down; the sales force stepped up its travel schedule; and the only thing on anyone's mind was "get those numbers up." Within a couple of months, no one was talking about the mission. Objectives, action plans, and time lines were all put on the back burner; and there they stayed forever. The mission died. Cause of death: neglect. Consequence: Trust died with it.

Company B was a large corporation with a board of directors and many stockholders. It had a new president who had very clear ideas about where he wanted to take the company and the legacy he wished to leave for the next generation. He knew that turning a company of this size around was like making a U-turn with the Queen Mary, so he began to put the pieces in place very slowly. In concert with the corporate planning process, he asked each of the company's divisions to create its own five-year plan, which was later meshed with the larger corporate plan. Based on what surfaced in that process, the president appointed several committees from the executive management team to study key elements and make recommendations.

Strategic planning is a time-intensive process, especially when the CEO sincerely seeks input from lower levels of the organization. When the corporate and division plans were finalized, the president spent some time studying them and comparing them to his personal vision. There was a surprisingly good match between where the divisions wanted to go and where he wanted to go. Since each division's plan incorporated the input of all levels of its own management, the planning process had extended deep into the organization and included the thoughts of many people.

The president put the combined vision in very rough form, had the wording polished by the communication department, and called a meeting of his executive team. The purpose of the meeting was to present the vision to the top people in the organization; give them plenty of time and freedom to react to it, change it, throw it out, or adopt it; and, finally, to embrace it as their own. It was a spirited, candid, tell-it-like-it-is meeting. While everyone knew the president was 100 percent committed to this vision, he did nothing to impose it on them.

The executive management team broke into committees and went off to hammer out various aspects of the vision. Then the whole team debated their conclusions. After two days of intense work, the final vision was adopted, standing committees were appointed, and the real work began. Each member of the executive team went back to his or her division, department, or work group and repeated the whole process with its top management. The president made an appearance at every meeting, enthusiastically selling his vision, but assuring everyone that it was not yet final and that their input would be seriously considered.

When that process was completed, the executive team took one more long look at the vision as it stood now and ratified it. Then it was communicated to the next level of management. In the meantime, preparations were underway for a corporate-wide rollout of the vision, which was now etched in stone. Following the rollout, there were to be six months of intense communication and activity to incorporate the vision into the very fabric of the corporate culture.

The communication department created tangible emblems and mementos to make the vision something employees could see and touch and feel, as well as hear about. The president didn't want a lot of razzle dazzle, but he did want employees to know this was serious business. As all that was going on, the committees continued to meet; and plans were fleshed out for getting the message out to the employees and other key audiences, including customers. Behind-the-scenes excitement was building, though only those directly involved knew anything about the plans.

As the pieces came together, practically on the eve of the big day, the president received a phone call that stopped the show. The company had been acquired by a competitor. In the space of a phone call, it had become a whole new ball game. He called his executive team together to make the announcement. There was a stunned silence. "What happens to the vision?" was one of the first questions. "The vision is dead," said the president. "There will be no rollout."

For the majority of employees of this company, this was not a big disappointment because they had no idea of what had been transpiring during the past two years. They wouldn't miss a vision they didn't know existed. But for those who did know, who had helped to shape it, who were committed to its potential, who shared the president's dream, something of great significance had died and, with it, the trust that life ever works out according to plan.

Company C was a family-owned manufacturing company that had been born in a kitchen and grew up to be a very successful enterprise. Its management style could only be described as "seat of the pants"; but, whatever it was called, it worked until the company put a product on the market that *didn't* work. The product had been rushed to market to meet customer demands and, as a result, had not gone through the rigorous testing that was ordinarily required. Sales plummeted and morale along with them.

The first order of business was to fix the problem; the second, to reverse the consequences. Management knew it had to get sales back up, but frankly no one knew exactly how to accomplish that in the present climate. The new vice-president of operations, who was not a member of the family, felt that the company needed a marketing plan. The management team, which consisted of only two other people— the president and the vice-president of sales—wholeheartedly agreed and promised to write one. Months went by, and nothing happened.

As a last resort, at the suggestion of the vice-president of operations, a marketing consultant was brought in to help create the plan. That decision marked the beginning of a series of events no one could have foreseen. The consultant was given free rein to gather all the information she needed from any and all sources. When she finished interviewing everyone from the chairman of the company (the founder and the president's father) to workers on the line and from distributors of the company's products to sales people and customers, the consultant had more questions than answers. She requested a meeting with the management team.

As an impartial outsider, she was asked to facilitate the meeting, which lasted for two days. It only took a few hours for the management team to come to the startling conclusion that, if they continued to run the company as they had been running it, they would quite literally run it right into the ground. First, they were stunned; then, they rolled up their sleeves and tackled the problem head on.

At the end of two days characterized by candor and confrontation of tough issues, they emerged with a company mission, a vision, and ten strategic objectives. The mission was a simple statement of why they were in business; the vision delineated how they wished to be perceived by all of those who had an interest and a stake in their success; and the strategic objectives were what they felt it would take to make the first two happen. This was, in many ways, a revolutionary step for this company.

The meeting was followed by the drafting of the long-awaited marketing plan. All of this was accomplished as a collaborative effort between the management team and the consultant. When the plan was in final form, the next challenge was to sell it to the board (the other members of the family). A very comprehensive presentation was prepared and presented; discussion among family members progressed from adversarial to skeptical to enthusiastic. At the end of the day, the board approved the plan with a few minor modifications.

The next step was a carefully orchestrated rollout to the next level of management, which took place at the first-ever management dinner, held at a very posh restaurant. All three members of the management team made short speeches from the perspectives of their individual areas of responsibility. Questions were welcomed; discussion was encouraged. The managers signed on.

It all looked great on paper; and, at the management level, excitement had taken hold. The challenge, of course, was communicating all of this to employees and other stakeholders. But that would only be step one. Step two would be actually putting it into practice. This little company was faced with unprecedented change. The whole endeavor would live or die on how they dealt with and helped others deal with change. This was much more than an exercise; if they failed, inevitably, the company would fail.

The management team engaged the services of a training firm that specialized in helping organizations work through the change process. Members of the board and all managers were the first to go through the program. Two promising and committed young men were certified to conduct the training. Every person in the company went through the program, which engaged them in the process of bringing the mission and vision to life and translating the corporate objectives into tangible actions.

With the vice-president of operations overseeing the process, things changed—slowly at first—and then momentum began to build. The first year was devoted to "putting their house in order." The marketing plan was implemented; internal teams were formed and empowered; sales reps were asked for their input; distributors and key customers were personally visited by the president; testing procedures were tightened; higher standards were set and met; and ISO 9001 certification was achieved.

Internally, there was constant fine tuning of processes and procedures. The first round of change training was followed by a second and then a third. Every six months, the management team met with the marketing consultant for a long, tough day of evaluating progress on the strategic objectives and the marketing plan. Together, they reviewed what they had hoped to achieve by this date, their present status on each item, where they expected to be six months down the road, and what specific actions would be required to get there.

In the midst of all of this activity, no one ever took their eyes off the vision. Week after week, month after month, they continued to make adjustments as they worked toward their objectives. Over time, some objectives were reached, a few were scrapped, and the rest became works in progress. This process is alive and well to this day. Employee involvement remains high. The vision is slowly becoming a reality. Momentum continues to build. And, bottom line, trust in the leaders and future of the company grows stronger every day.

Conclusion

These are three very real examples of how the crafting of a company vision can create, sustain, or destroy the fragile element of trust. In the first case, the culprit was management's lack of commitment to seeing the process through the rough times. In the second case, the company's leadership was prepared to walk the walk; but, unforeseen, outside forces brought the whole project to a screeching halt. In the third case, the difficult, step-by-step process of creating a vision, putting the necessary pieces in place, and following through in all the critical ways did happen and is still happening.

It takes effort and vigilance to plant the seeds of trust, nurture them as they grow, and carefully protect them during harvest time. But it is worth the effort. Trust is the foundation upon which relationships are built. It is what sets great leaders apart from mediocre ones. It provides a safe environment for creativity and risk taking. Ultimately, it is the glue that holds organizations together.

SECTION TWO

Dealing With Difficult Situations

CHAPTER SIX

Understanding Your Corporate Culture

Renee Broussard has experienced three very different business cultures within a brief period of time: a privately held company, a publicly traded Fortune *100 corporation, and the not-for-profit organization where she now works. While she has had little difficulty making the transition from one to another, she is finding it a challenge to figure out the players, the rules of the game, and which moves to make in her new position.*

I interpret corporate culture as the basic setup of an organization—the structure, the hierarchy, the politics, the jockeying for position. It takes time to learn a new corporate culture. Coming in as a new person makes it very difficult for me to figure out who to trust. When I get conflicting information I don't know who to believe or where all these people fit.

My present company places disabled people in employable situations. We test them for conversational abilities, interests, physical restrictions, and dexterity, so that we can give them realistic goals. We deal with any kind of disability—physical, mental, developmental, emotional, and addictive. Our clients are all referrals from various state agencies.

I am coordinating a brand new program in which we place people with disabilities in apprenticeships in the community for three to twelve months. Placements are based on their interests and supported by testing. The program was originally designed for learning-disabled individuals who do not do well in classroom settings. This is real-world stuff. Our clients are paid minimum wage, as opposed to working for nothing. This makes them feel valued and allows them to survive.

I was hired because of my marketing background. Yet, I'm really coming in with my own disability, which is lack of knowledge of the system. I have no social service background. I'm not familiar with their terminology—all the acronyms. If you don't know the jargon, you miss the whole thrust of what people are talking about. I feel really comfortable about asking, *What does that mean?* And they are all very understanding and more than willing to explain.

I've been there about three months. If I were to describe the culture, I would say it's fabulous. It's a social service agency. There are a lot of young people, perhaps in their first positions, as well as more mature individuals who have moved up in the hierarchy or the corporate world. They are loving, caring, warm, supportive, and very nurturing—not just to the clients, but to each other and to me, as a newcomer.

In my last job, I was contracted to a *Fortune* 100 company. I worked with people in the marketing area who designed programs for marketing a particular product. My company, out of New York City, was contracted to recruit and hire "reps" and to provide support for them. It was my job to be sure they got what they needed to do the job. It was like a triangle. I worked for one company, spent my time at another company, and managed a field sales force that belonged to neither company.

The client organization had a number of divisions. In the division where I worked, the people were well educated, well dressed, and very "preppy." I often thought how lucky I was to be working with such an elite, cultured, intellectual group. I'm finding that the people at my new company are all of that and more but just not into the same values. The corporate folks were more concerned with appearances—looking right, saying the right things, being associated with the right corporation.

Social workers have degrees, too. In fact, many of them have Masters degrees; but they are less interested in the trappings of life and more concerned with getting the job done and helping clients.

I find this very appealing because I wanted to do something that really counted. In my last job, I was a counselor to my "reps." When something went wrong, they'd call me, and I would sometimes think, This is not life and death; it's *a product*. But in my job now, we are really shaping people's lives and giving them opportunities to grow and become worthwhile and productive. We are trying to move the roadblocks out of their lives and to help them develop their purpose and dignity.

The company I worked for in New York went through a dramatic culture change while I was there. It was one of the reasons I left, in fact. When I joined the company, it was a family-type, low-key organization made up mostly of women. The stress level was low; the environment was very supportive. The president was a real "lady" and, at the same time, a very good businesswoman. When she retired, about midway through my tenure, things started to change.

The woman who took over the reins—also a "lady" but more competitive and ambitious—told us we could not remain small and survive. Since then, the company has grown tremendously, and the stress level has risen proportionately. Twenty-five percent of the workforce is now male. Workaholism, competition, and fighting for survival have become the new way of life.

The former owner sent birthday cards to every one of the five hundred reps. There are now probably more than *five thousand* reps. The caliber of client companies and the benefits to the reps have deteriorated. When I left, my job was divided up among three people, each dividing their attention among a variety of client accounts. The "reps" no longer receive the individual attention I had been able to give them.

It was not my choice to leave my last job. I knew what I was doing so well, I could have done it in my sleep. Yet, it was time to move on. I knew that. I had worked for seventeen uninterrupted years, and I felt I deserved a sabbatical. I took almost nine months off before I went back to work. This job sort of fell in my lap, and I felt it was meant to be.

I heard a talk on leaving corporate America and going into not for profit. I thought, *This is exactly the way I feel.* The company I worked for had changed completely. The company I was contracted to was downsizing. Many of those who remained were doing the work of three people. Most of my friends there were stressed out. I thought corporate America was very dysfunctional, and I wanted to get out of it.

Other than the insecurity of not knowing the social service business or the players, I actually have had a rather easy time moving into this new culture. But I'm being very cautious. I don't want to make a mistake or burn any bridges. Actually, I don't know how I'm doing because I'm not getting much training or feedback. It has been an experiential learning process, much like the apprenticeships I develop, where one learns by doing. My boss keeps saying, *You're this close ... you're this close.* But close to *what*?

*   *   *

When Thoreau observed that "the mass of men lead lives of quiet desperation," he might well have been describing life in corporate America. Of course, not everyone is unhappy in his or her job; but, unfortunately, many people are. For them, facing each day is tough; getting through it, even tougher. Friday is greeted with a sigh of relief; but the weekend seems to fly by, often filled with the catch-up chores and errands that didn't get accomplished during the week.

Why are so many employees—at all levels of their companies—unhappy, unsatisfied, and unfulfilled? Is it what they do or where they do it? Are they under-performing or merely unqualified? And, if they are so miserable, why don't they just leave and find another job? The questions may be simple, but the answers are anything but.

There are countless reasons why people are disgruntled at work, including those already mentioned and many more. Unless a person has a substantial nest egg, a winning lottery ticket, or a better job waiting in the wings, he or she is not likely to say, "Take this job and shove it," no matter how bad it is. That isn't practical in a market in which companies are laying off workers in astonishing numbers, and people are being offered early retirement packages when they are far too young to retire and too old to find a comparable position.

So, most remain in jobs that don't challenge them enough; that demand more than they can deliver; remain in situations where they are underpaid or, strange as it may seem, *over*paid and trapped by *golden handcuffs;* remain in dead-end positions or in higher-level ones in which they are clearly ineffective and bound to fail.

If the Shoe Fits ...

Do any of these scenarios describe your predicament? Are you one of those who leads a life of quiet desperation or, worse yet, one of unmistakable discontent? Do you consider your job one of life's non-negotiable bad deals instead of a source of satisfaction, as well as income?

It doesn't take a rocket scientist to know how you feel about your job. If you are unhappy, no one knows it better than you do. But what you may *not* know is the cause of your unhappiness. This is not something you can afford to ignore. If you understand the real reasons behind your discontent, you will be in a much better position to take constructive action. If you don't, the problem will persist and possibly intensify.

The Power of the Workplace

Of the many underlying causes of job dissatisfaction, one is simply *where you work.* That encompasses the physical environment; the location in relation to your home; and, perhaps most important, the culture of your organization. Up until 1982, when Terrence E. Deal and Allan A. Kennedy wrote a book called *Corporate Cultures: The Rites and Rituals of Corporate Life,* no one had even heard of the concept of "corporate culture." Deal and Kennedy literally coined the phrase, which has since become an accepted part of business vernacular.

In 1982, however, the idea of every organization being an identifiable, influential, and ongoing micro-society within the larger macrosociety of the business world was a startling one. The dictionary definition of culture is, "The integrated pattern of human behavior that includes thought, speech, action, and artifacts ... ." A less formal definition of corporate culture was offered by Marvin Bower, former managing director of McKinsey & Company and author of *The Will to*

Manage. Bower described it as "the way we do things around here." Deal and Kennedy took it one step further, interpreting corporate culture as "a cohesion of values, myths, heroes, and symbols that have come to mean a great deal to the people who work [in a given organization."

It is people who are the heart of any culture and people who make business work. "Culture," wrote Deal and Kennedy, "ties people together and gives meaning and purpose to their day-to-day lives." If the place you work is a toxic or dysfunctional environment, the meaning it brings to your life may be negative and harmful to your health—mental, as well as physical.

Why does it matter? It matters because there are spoken and unspoken rules for getting along in any community, including the workplace. If you don't catch the cues or understand them, even when you do get them, you will be out of step with the beat to which everyone else around you is marching. That's why it is so important to step back and take an objective look at the world in which you spend so much of your time.

Since most of us are not trained to accomplish such a task, here is a step-by-step guidebook for how to go about it. A good way to begin is by adopting the attitude of an *ethnologist*—someone who studies societies, how they developed, how people behave within them, what rules govern such behavior, and how they are similar and different from other societies.

Peeling the Onion

This process is not as overwhelming as it may seem, though it will take some time and effort to go through the steps. The trick is to begin with the obvious and work through the layers to the less than obvious. Think of peeling away the layers of an onion, one layer at a time. Each layer represents an aspect of your company, from gross to subtle. Authors Deal and Kennedy put it this way: "The process begins at the surface and proceeds inward, toward the company's unconscious." The first step on your culture study, then, would be just to look around you at your physical surroundings.

Start with the outside of your building. If your company owns it, its architecture was undoubtedly intended to make a statement. What kind of impression did you get when you first saw it, and has that impression changed? If your company rents space, rather than owning the building, appearance is no less of an issue. If this is one of many sites around the city or the country, is there a consistency of look to all of them? If this is the headquarters of a large corporation, what do the other locations look like? Do they meet the same standards, or are they rather like poor relations? And what does all this tell you?

The outside of building is like the clothes you wear: It provides a first and often indelible impression. If headquarters is first class but branch offices, plants, and other facilities are second class, or even a bit shabby by comparison, you might assume that form takes precedence over function. If the executive wing has plush carpets and polished wood, while every other work area has tile floors and metal desks, you know who is considered most important. You also have your first clue about the culture as a whole: It is hierarchical.

Inside the front door, you are most familiar with your own floor and work area, of course. Is the pecking order so obvious that you could probably figure out everybody's organizational status by the size, location, decor, and art work in his or her office or cubicle—even if you didn't work there? If so, power counts here. So do the accouterments of power. At the other extreme is the more egalitarian, open-office setting, where everybody has a cubicle, including the president; and no one uses real estate as a privilege of rank. In such a setting, the culture supports a flat organizational structure that emphasizes no frills, productivity, and open communication.

Mixed Messages

Companies reveal a great deal about their cultures, intention-ally or unintentionally, through their formal communications. Everything from annual reports and press releases to internal memos and meetings speak volumes. Strong cultures identify, publicize, and attempt to live their core values. Weak cultures write about their achievements, results, or profits, steering clear of such "touchy-feely" subjects as values.

Many companies publish mission and vision statements. Some result from employee input; others are handed down from the executive office. Often they hang, beautifully framed, on walls throughout the building; or there is an icon on everyone's desk, proudly displaying the mission. If your company has such a set of guiding principles, are they just words on a wall, or are they part of the fabric of "how we do things around here?" In other words, do your executives and coworkers walk the walk? In cultures that are "all of a piece," they do.

The next layer of your symbolic onion is the reception area, a veritable treasure trove of information. Note the decor and how it broadcasts what your company stands for, even if that has never been articulated. Notice such things as whether the receptionist is typing, opening mail, or stuff-ing envelopes, as well as taking calls. If so, your culture val-ues *productivity.* "Time is money. Don't just sit around wait-ing for the phone to ring; *do something,*" is the unspoken message.

Does the receptionist hang up visitors' coats, offer cof-fee, and escort them to their appointments? If so, you can infer that guests are important, and service is paramount. Or, does she give them a visitor's pass and ask them to sign a guest register? If she does so, yours is a bureaucratic organi-zation that values security. Does she look like she just stepped out of Vogue, telling you that appearance counts, or more like dress-down Friday, which says, it's not how you *look* but what you *do* that counts?

Racing With the Clock

Remember the "time study man" from the musical, *Pajama Game,* singing, "Can't waste time … can't waste time … when you're racing with the clock … ." How *do* people spend their time in your company? The answer tells you a great deal about where the culture focuses its energy. An externally focused company, for example, will stay close the marketplace and the customer, always ready to turn on a dime if that's what is required. On the other hand, an internally focused company—because it is watching what's going on inside the business—is likely to be slower to anticipate a changing business climate and respond to it, let alone prepare for it in advance.

Research Is the Key

Finally, just talk to people. Ask questions. Ask about the company's history, even if you know it. Chances are what you hear won't be accurate, but that doesn't really matter. What matters is that you are hearing the *mythology* of the company, which is one of the elements that helps define the culture. Ask peers if they consider the company successful and, if so, why? The answers will tell you a lot about your company's values.

Ask how employees are viewed, and you'll learn what kind of person can really make it in this company. Ask people how they feel about working here. You'll get an earful about what is expected, whether management's actions parallel their words, the rituals everyone knows about but no one ever mentions, and dozens of other open secrets.

Be a snoop. Read everything that comes your way. Observe the dynamics of company meetings. Watch the process. Listen for who talks, about what, and to whom. Take note of the stories you hear around the coffee machine. Listen between the lines of what people say for what they really mean. Notice who gets promoted and who gets fired. See how long people stay and what, if any, are the rewards for hanging in there. Ultimately, you will uncover patterns that are so clear you'll wonder how you missed them before.

Survival of the Fittest

There are two classifications of corporate cultures: strong and weak. Once you know what to look for and how to assess what you find, you will have no difficulty identifying which is which. According to the originators of this concept, strong cultures have the following characteristics.

They believe in something. They have a guiding philosophy and a value system. They share them with employees; they live them; and they expect every else to do so.

They have informal rules that tell people what is expected of them. These rules are reinforced by "heroes" who symbolize the core values of the company. They have "rituals" or planned activities that give everyone in the company a chance to develop an *esprit de corps*. They care about their employees, and they demonstrate that concern in myriad ways. The bottom line, say Dean and Kennedy is that "a strong culture enables people to feel better about what they do, so that they are more likely to work harder."

Weak cultures, on the other hand, are almost the polar opposite. They lack clear values and in one way or another have trouble nailing down what it takes to be successful in their particular business. On the other hand, when strong beliefs *are* present, they often vary from one part of the company to another. There is no definitive "way we do things around here." Either everyone marches to his or her own drummer or some people do things one way and other people do them just the opposite way. If you study a weak culture, you'll have a hard time finding the cohesive patterns that define it.

Two of the marks of seasoned ethnologists are their ability to observe what is right in front of them, without coloring it with their own judgments, and their reluctance to jump to conclusions too early in the game. Unscrambling the subtleties of a complex culture takes time, attention to detail, and a sense of the hidden patterns in what seems like chaos.

Why Bother?

There are many reasons to take the time to go through this analytical process. If you don't understand your culture, intellectually or intuitively, you are going to spend your entire time there going "up the down staircase." You just won't get it. You'll always be one beat off. This is not to say that conformity is to be revered or "the organization man" to be the role model he was in the fifties. But there *is* a rhythm to life in every company that allows you to fit in and feel at home. When you are out of sync with that rhythm, there is added stress in your life; and, when you are downright miserable, that stress is multiplied many times over.

The American Heart Association defines stress as "the bodily or mental tension that results from a person's response to physical, chemical, or emotional factors." Everyone experiences stress, but they do so to different degrees and react to it in different ways. While it is almost impossible to measure the effect of emotional or psychological stress on the body, there is much evidence that stress plays a part in coronary heart disease, strokes, cancer, arthritis, eating disorders, gastrointestinal problems, depression, skin eruptions, and autoimmune diseases.

The Framingham Heart Study found that women in clerical positions have twice as many heart attacks as do homemakers. It wasn't the *work* that affected their risk of heart attack but rather the *amount of control* these women felt they had in their lives. Those who were at the greatest risk of heart attack were most likely to harbor suppressed hostility, to hold jobs that gave them little chance for advancement, and to feel frustration in situations over which they had little or no influence.

Both men and women are at greater risk of heart disease if they are aggressive, angry, hostile, and cynical. The American Heart Association's literature points out that *the way you respond to your environment* is significant and offers this advice: "Evaluate your lifestyle, your job satisfaction, and your physical and emotional response to stressful events. Do what you can to manage or reduce the stressful factors in your home and your workplace. And take active steps to gain a sense of control in your life."

That is very good advice because, if you don't work through your emotional distress and do continue to bury your feelings, you run the risk of compromising your immune and endocrine systems. Autoimmune diseases, such as rheumatoid arthritis, multiple sclerosis, some thyroid disorders, and lupus are all caused in part by autoimmunity. Studies have also shown that stress helps trigger a dormant herpes virus and Epstein Barr, the virus associated with chronic fatigue syndrome.

The Bottom Line

If you are experiencing a sense of hopelessness or despair and view your situation as out of your control, ultimately it is your immune system that will suffer. In fact, if this situation persists, it can literally numb the cells of your body to the point where they would be incapable of destroying cancer cells or bacteria. What is important to remember is that it is not stress itself that creates immune system problems; it is *the perception that the stress is inescapable*—that there is nothing you can do about it—that causes your immune system to shut down.

It's no secret that there are many more women in the workforce than ever before and that women are encountering many of the health and safety hazards traditionally experienced by men. These include exposure to dangerous work environments and the increased likelihood of car or plane accidents as women travel more. Working outside the home also tends to place women under additional stress because the vast majority of them still face cooking, cleaning, and child-rearing responsibilities when they get home at night.

The good news is that women seem to deal with the stresses of life in a healthier, more life-enhancing way than do their male counterparts. "As a group," writes Author Robin Marantz Henig, in *How a Woman Ages,* "women are more likely than men to express their emotions and seek out psychological support from professionals, friends, and family. Because of the contribution that stress makes to many degenerative diseases, some observers believe that a woman's tendency to work through her problems—compared to a man's tendency to bottle them up inside—might help contribute to her greater life expectancy."

The bad news is that many women are turning to cigarettes, alcohol, prescription drugs, tranquilizers, caffeine, and saccharin-laden diet drinks to relieve their stress. This, of course, puts them in the same risk category as men and increases their chances for heart attacks and strokes.

Since stress is not a new phenomenon, there is an abundance of literature available on how to combat it in ways that are far more health promoting than smoking, drinking, and popping pills. Exercise leads the list—especially cardiovascular exercise, such as walking, running, bicycling, roller blading, skating, swimming, cross country skiing, dancing, and anything that keeps your heart pumping steadily for at least 30 minutes.

You can hardly pick up a magazine today without finding at least one article on how to minimize the stress in your life. While these publications all extol the virtues of getting your body in motion, they are also suggesting that you get your mind to *stop* moving. Meditation, prayer, music, and painting are all ways to still the mind and calm the soul.

Conclusion

Stress is a fact of life. It will always exist. The point is that it is not the circumstances of your life or job that create stress; it is your *perception and interpretation* of those circumstances. If you allow yourself to crumble with everything that happens, you are literally shortening your life. Someone captured that concept nicely in a book title that asked: *Is It Worth Dying For?*

Working for a living puts you in daily contact with situations that can make you feel helpless, hostile, alienated, frustrated, and quite literally sick. There are many effective ways of coping with those feelings, from getting on the treadmill to seeing a counselor. One way to prevent unnecessary dissatisfaction, despair, or depression and the stress that inevitably follows is to examine the underlying cause of your discomfort and take steps to eliminate it.

Are you in the right job, in the right company? Are you and your present corporate culture a mismatch or a marriage made in heaven? Are your problems job related, the result of a people issue, or completely separate from the nine-to-five part of your day? Step back. Take a look. Take your time. Talk to a friend. Talk to a therapist. Be objective and honest with yourself. Figure it out, and then do what you have to do. Whatever the underlying cause, surely it is *not* worth dying for. Few things are.

CHAPTER SEVEN

Functioning in a Dysfunctional Company

Katherine Jarvice *is manager of human resources for a manufacturing division of a midwestern* Fortune *100 company. She began her career with the company as a secretary, worked her way up through the ranks, skipping several salary grades along the way, and was named to a newly created position she helped to design. Along the way, she went back to school for a bachelor's degree in human resources management, followed immediately by a master's in organizational communications.*

To me, a dysfunctional work environment is one that culturally, socially, and morally goes against everything I believe in. Of course, no company sets out to be dysfunctional. They just do what they've done for years and years. Those things work for them, so they keep doing them.

My company has just named a new corporate vice-president of human resources. He's a good old boy who has been with us for a long time. I mentioned to my boss that putting an old timer in that job doesn't allow for any new ideas and innovative thinking.

His response was, "Why do we need new ideas and innovative thinking? We have done very well with this thinking for many years. Why should we change it?" My boss has been with the company for twenty years. He came up though the ranks, and he has bought in. He's what I call a "lifer."

We were a lean, mean machine long before it became fashionable. We've always been downsized. There are so many things that have to be done and never enough time to do them. Everyone's job is twice as big as it should be. I met with our HR group; and we decided to concentrate on those things we know we can do, that will most benefit the employees, without having to get permission or approval from the next level up. As little as these things may seem, employees need them. That's how my department survives in a dysfunctional organization.

Here's how I would describe the value system here: There are two kinds of car buyers. The first is the person who buys a new car and says, "I'm going to wash this car. I'm going to take care of it like a baby, and it's going to last me a long time." And he washes it, and he waxes it, and he changes the oil, and he talks to the car, and he treats it with love and tenderness. To repay him, the car lasts for ten years, maybe longer.

The second is the person who buys a new car and says, "I'm going to buy this car, but then I'm not going to put any money into it. I'm not going to fuss with it. I'm going to run it until it dies, and then I'll buy a new one."

This company is like the second person. We "buy" an employee and work her until she's used up. Then, we throw her away. When the employee has had enough, she leaves; and the company says, "O.K. we'll find another one." I think *that's* dysfunctional.

Because everyone has so much on their plates, work issues take precedence over people issues. Managers don't seem to realize that by *not* dealing with the people issues they lose productivity, and they end up with not only poor *quantity* but also poor *quality* of work. People are disillusioned. They hate to come to work, and eventually they quit.

The biggest frustration I have is that I can't do more to make the environment better. Every people issue that a manager chooses not to handle or can't handle comes to me. Those run the gamut from complaints about the inappropriate length of an employee's skirt to the suspicion that someone has a substance-abuse problem.

Most managers feel if they ignore the problem it will go away. But when it gets so big that they can't ignore it, they bring it to me. Whether the problem is insignificant or major, it has an impact on the work environment. I treat all of them as equally important.

Our profits have increased every quarter for the last 36 years, and we will do anything to keep that record going. When the Asian crisis hit, in order to maintain our continuous profit, quarter after quarter, we were all put under a hiring freeze. Nobody could do anything because we had to offset the divisions that were being impacted by the Asian crisis.

Like a dysfunctional family that keeps its business to itself, no one really knows much about us except that we are stable and profitable. Our CEO is very well thought of because our company gives a lot of money to a lot of causes. Our public image is positive. We are leaders in the community ... *very* civic-minded.

To be a successful corporation, we *must* be civic-minded; so, we are civic-minded. Every division has a contribution quota that it must raise and give away. There is a *mandate* that we be philanthropic! We actually incentivize people to contribute to charitable causes. We have to give our employee something so that they will give something.

I think we all have to know what's important to us inside, in our souls and in our hearts. For me, it's important to greet every person I see by name with a big friendly hello. It's important to me because I think it's important to them. I have to identify what makes me feel like a whole person and then live it.

I deal with employees and managers at all levels, and I have found repeatedly that *people lie.* Not only do they hear what they want to hear, they tell you what they think *you* want to hear. They tell you things they think will make them look good. I consider it an important part of my job to very simply get to the real issues ... the truth behind the lies.

The only way I can survive in this environment is to look at the things I am able to accomplish and not look at the things I can't get done. I don't focus on failures or something I feel I haven't done well. If I disagree with a vice-president—whether it's on a hiring decision or a policy change or some small thing—ultimately, a VP outranks me. I'm going to lose. I don't take that personally anymore.

I was in a stress management session, and the instructor read the "Serenity Prayer" to us—the one with the line, *Give me the serenity to accept the things I cannot change.* Someone in the group remarked that, even when she did recognize the things she couldn't change, she still felt anxious and frustrated. The instructor pointed out to her that she had forgotten one important word in that line: *accept.* It is not enough to recognize what we can't do anything about; we have to *accept* it. What a breakthrough that was!

*   *   *

There is a lot of talk these days about the negative effects of growing up in a *dysfunctional family.* That phrase covers a wide range of problems, from anything short of fictionally perfect to the worst scenarios of neglect, abuse, and destruction one might conjure. One official definition is this: "… a family in which the emotional and physical support needed for individuation and healthy development are missing, and family members are sacrificed to the family group itself."

By simply changing a few words, that is also a perfect description of a *dysfunctional organization.* Try this on for size: "… a company in which the emotional and physical support needed for personal and professional development are missing and employees are sacrificed to the organization itself."

There isn't much difference between a sick family and a sick company. Both have damaging effects on everyone associated with them. Yet, it's not unusual for someone to grow up in an unhealthy home environment and be completely unaware of it. That is also true of unhealthy work environments. If you don't know you have a problem, it is, of course, impossible to solve it. That's why it is so important to understand the culture in which you work and the effect it is having on your health and emotional well-being.

The Way It Was; the Way It Is

A humorous definition of a dysfunctional family is any family with more than one person in it, implying that all families are dysfunctional in their own way. To some extent that's true, but what is considered healthy or sick varies with the times. In the fifties, the family portrayed in the television sitcom "Father Knows Best" was hailed as the ideal. Today, we would probably consider it paternalistic and autocratic. There are some who would even suggest that the father, played by Robert Young, was little more than a benevolent dictator.

What is considered a healthy or unhealthy organization has also changed over the years. The paternalistic model—in which the company took care of its employees and provided them with security, support, and discipline—is an anachronism. Long-term employment and employee loyalty have been replaced by early retirement packages, lay-offs, and job-hopping.

Change is the order of the day. Everything, it seems, is in a constant state of flux and transformation. The world is getting smaller. Corporations join together, split apart, restructure, go in and out of bankruptcy, and redefine their core businesses every day. The industrial revolution has given way to the technological revolution. Yet today's breakthroughs in technology are all but obsolete tomorrow. Manufacturing has been supplanted by the service industry. Communications are paramount, but that has led to information overload and complex ideas being reduced to thirty-second sound bytes. No wonder there are so many dysfunctional organizations.

How do you know if *your* organization is among them? What are symptoms of a sick company and, even more important, what are the consequences to you of working in one?

Symptoms

What follows is a list of symptoms of dysfunctional organizations. It is unlikely that any company will have all of them, since it would not survive. If you recognize half (ten) of these characteristics, your company is probably going around in circles, perhaps giving the impression of health, but already beginning to decay beneath the surface. If you can relate to three-quarters (15) of them, you can safely conclude that you work for a sick company.

- Communication is indirect, unclear, controlled, and often manipulated.
- Conflicts occur behind the scenes but are unacknowledged by those involved or by others.
- Decisions are made by small but powerful cliques.
- Dualistic thinking leads to people, actions, and decisions being judged as either good or bad.
- Employees lack direction on what is expected of them and how to behave.
- Information is disseminated by gossip, which gets people unduly excited or upset.
- Management is isolated, keeping employees in the dark about what's really going on.
- Meetings are long, tedious, unfocused, and unproductive.
- Much communication is by gossip.
- New polices and complex procedures are often announced in writing, then never clarified.
- Open expression of feelings is discouraged or ignored.
- Promises and rosy pictures of the future distract people from an unhappy present.
- Rather than seeking the *causes* of problems, management looks for scapegoats.
- Relationships and alliances are built on secrecy.
- Resistance to policies ranges from passive to overtly destructive.
- Risk is discouraged; making mistakes is not tolerated.

- The myths and rituals of the corporate culture are ignored and eventually forgotten.
- The mundane is overblown; significant issues are often minimized.
- When things go wrong, people blame each other.
- Workplace friendships rarely develop, or they are "nine-to-five" friendships of convenience.

This is by no means an exhaustive list. Dysfunctional organizations are also rigid and inflexible. Things are done as they've always been done; the rules don't change. People's needs are not met. Growth is stifled. Everyone knows there are problems and what those problems are, but no one talks about them or admits that things are not as they appear to be. Employees feel isolated from each other, from management, and from outside influences.

Dysfunctional organizations spend more time arguing over who did or didn't do something than they do getting anything accomplished. Things are either black or white, right or wrong. People take sides, polarizing them even more. Turnover is high; employee morale is low. Employees are suspicious of each other and even more so of management.

Addiction in the Workplace

One sure sign of dysfunction in the workplace is *addiction.* The dictionary defines addiction as "the state of physical or psychological dependence due to habitual consumption of a habit-forming substance." In today's world, the word has come to mean a craving for *anything* we want or need so much that we are powerless to resist it.

Authors Anne Wilson Schaef and Diane Fassel describe addiction as "any process or substance that begins to have control over us in such a way that we feel we must be dishonest with ourselves or others about it. Addiction leads us into increasing compulsiveness in our behavior," they write in *The Addictive Organization.* "If there is something we are not willing to give up in order to make our lives fuller or more healthy, it probably can be classified as an addiction."

Addiction is reaching epidemic proportions in our society. In fact, it is difficult to find anyone who is not addicted to something, whether that something is a substance, a behavior, a process, or another person. It is no surprise, then, that "many of our organizations are addictive organizations embedded in an addictive society," observe Schaef and Fassel, who have identified four forms of addiction in the business world. They are those in which:

- A key person in the company is an addict.
- Addicted employees recreate their family situations in the workplace.
- The organization is the addictive substance.
- The organization is the addict.

Addicts, Children of Addicts, and Codependents

There is no question that the leader or any pivotal person in a company exerts tremendous influence on the corporate culture; the attitudes of employees; the way things get done and decisions are made; and, ultimately, the success or failure of the business. When that person is an active addict, the results can be disastrous. For one thing, addiction is a contagious disease. To work in an addictive workplace almost assures that you and everyone else will become ill in one way or another.

Executives don't have a lock on addiction, of course. People at any level of a company can be addicts, and they certainly bring all of the trappings of their disease to work. "Alcoholics can and often repeat at work some of the same behaviors they exhibit at home," note Schaef and Fassel. They lie, they intimidate, they create chaos, and they make poor judgments, to name just a few of those behaviors. They hide their disease, and others help them in hiding it. Alcoholism and many other addictions are not only progressive; they are deadly. Untreated addiction cannot be hidden forever.

Experts at coping with and perpetuating an addictive environment are adult children of alcoholics, better known as ACAs. On the surface, these people are anything but disruptive. Their drugs of choice are workaholism and perfectionism—two behaviors that are encouraged, rather than discouraged in the business world. They never fail to come through in a crisis because their entire lives have consisted of one crisis after another. They don't fall apart while everything around them is doing so; but they do become unglued at their own tiniest mistakes, drowning in a barrage of self-criticism. Another name for ACAs is *codependents.*

Addicts could not survive without codependents to make excuses for them, cover for them, and "enable" their behavior. Codependents smooth out the rough edges of the addict's life, keep unbearable situations bearable for everyone, and perpetuate circumstances that should be confronted and stopped. Like addicts, codependents are caught in a vicious cycle of excuses denial, secrecy, and lies. Because addiction, no matter what its object, adversely affects everyone it touches, codependents, too, are sick.

"Acceptable" and Invisible Addictions

One of the most dangerous facets of an addictive organization is when loyalty to the organization substitutes for living one's own life and the *organization* becomes the addictive substance. An addictive organization is like a family in which everyone knows what is expected of them and plays by the rules. In such an environment, work is the top priority; everything else pales by comparison.

In its most extreme form, the addiction turns into *workaholism,* an insidious and often fatal disease, according to researchers Schaef and Fassel, who found much evidence of societal support for and, in fact, *admiration* of, this lifestyle. Women's magazines, particularly, extol the virtues of working beyond any reasonable limits and juggling a husband, children, exercise, and a bustling social life as a sign of "having it all." The workaholic, say Schaef and Fassel, becomes addicted to the process of work, using it as a fix to get ahead, be successful, avoid feeling, and escape from real life. Work is like a drug, producing a high—a surge of adrenalin—that nothing else equals.

Organizations are not only the source of people's addictions, they can be addicts in their own right. When you think of the characteristics of active addicts, this begins to make more sense. Addicts have no control over their addictive behavior. They cut themselves off from the help and advice of family and friends. As they become more chaotic internally, they try to exert more control over their external world. Their thinking is muddled, fearful, and often irrational. That description could just as easily fit an addicted person, corporation, or entire society.

The Road to Recovery

An addictive organization affects everyone in and around it: employees and their families; customers and suppliers; shareholders, if it is publicly traded; and the community or communities in which it operates. If addiction in any of its forms is a problem where you work, you cannot afford to live in a state of denial. It's important to remember that addictions are progressive and often fatal, whether it is a person or a corporation that is afflicted.

If it is a person, there are many resources to call upon in the recovery process, from treatment centers for substance abuse problems to twelve-step programs for virtually any addiction. Twelve-step programs are all based on the original Alcoholics Anonymous (AA) model, which has proved not only effective but life-saving for many people at all stages of their disease. AA and all twelve-step programs are support groups that provide a safe and loving environment for people to relinquish their addictive behaviors, go through the recovery process, and begin to rebuild their lives.

Organizational recovery is more complicated, though many of the principles of twelve-step programs do work in a business environment. An addicted or addictive organization is sick, and the sicker it gets, the less its management is likely to admit it. When an entire company enables addictive behavior and lives in denial, the disease will progress unchecked until the company can no longer function.

The big question of course is, *What can you, as one person, do about all of this?* Though bringing about any change may seem like a daunting task, there are some things you can do. First, try to remember that one person *can* have an impact on a larger institution. There are many examples of a single individual changing the destiny of a nation or the course of history. It is certainly not out of the question.

If *you* are addicted to a substance, a destructive behavior, your job, or your company—or if you have a close association with someone who is an addict—there is obviously something you can do about your own recovery. If your company has an Employee Assistance Program (EAP), that's a very good place to begin. An EAP provides confidential counseling on a wide range of problems, including addictions, and can help you directly or refer you to the best resource for your particular situation. If your addiction is to alcohol or drugs, your own physician is another good starting point, as well as a referral source for treatment if that is necessary.

If the addict is the president of your company, some other key executive, or another employee, the situation becomes more complex. Much of what you will be able to do depends upon your position in the company. If you are a manager or supervisor, you have a little more latitude than if the person you want to help is at a higher level than you are. *Intervention* is the most acceptable method of helping an addict move toward treatment, a twelve-step program, and recovery; but conducting an intervention is something you should do with help from an EAP counselor, someone trained in this process, or a higher-level executive who knows what he or she is doing. Don't try it alone because, despite your best intentions, it could backfire.

Facilitating the recovery process for an entire company is a tough, but not necessarily impossible, job. Education about addiction, the addictive process, and addictive organizations is an essential element. Often, people within the company do recognize that there is a problem and often can even describe it. What they may not know is that the problem is part of the bigger picture of addiction or what to do about it. Knowing that it has a name and that it is not unique to their particular organization can help management begin to deal with it.

"Dealing with it," of course, involves coming out of denial and taking a good, hard look at the corporate culture; how decisions are made and carried out; what is valued, how people are treated; and all the policies and procedures that support those things. This is probably not going to happen without top management's buy-in and support. And even if your company's leadership does embrace the need for scrutiny and change, understand that this will be a long, hard process that can only be accomplished over time.

While you, as a lone individual, have far more ability to affect your addictive organization than you may realize, at best, it won't be easy; at worst, it may not even be possible. This prayer recited at the beginning of every twelve-step meeting is the best attitude you can bring to your efforts:

> *God, give me the serenity to accept the things I*
> *cannot change, the courage to change the things*
> *I can, and the wisdom to know the difference.*

Violence in the Workplace

The most extreme manifestation of a dysfunctional organization is workplace violence, which is one of the leading causes of death in this country. According to the January, 1997 issue of *USA Today Magazine,* "Crime, harassment, and internal violence are becoming commonplace at work. Recent figures from the National Institute for Occupational Safety and Health (NIOSH) and the Bureau of Labor Statistics show that people at work are increasingly exposed to lethal violence ... The majority of incidents are not fatal assaults but everyday occurrences of physical violence, verbal threats, and forms of harassment."

Violence cuts across all business segments, areas of the country, company size, and public or private sectors. It is not, as many people believe, limited to irate employees or ex-employees venting their frustration with a gun. In fact, it is much broader than that, taking the form of:

- fighting between two employees
- verbal intimidation by an employee or supervisor
- threatening letters, notes, e-mail, or faxes
- vandalism of company or employee property
- possession of weapons on company property
- physical assault

Causes and Costs of Violence

There is no single factor that contributes to violence in a work environment. Rather, there is a set of conditions that, taken together, create the climate for violence to erupt. Those conditions include:

- paranoid personality and thinking
- a sense of helplessness, hopelessness, and isolation
- some precipitating event, such as losing a job or changing jobs, sexual or some other kind of harassment, or what is perceived as an unwelcome policy change
- ignoring the needs of employees and early warning signals of violence
- being unprepared, caught off guard, and reacting inadequately to violent occurrences

Violence at work is costly to victims, witnesses, companies, and communities. Victims of violence often suffer from post-traumatic syndrome and any number of trauma-related illnesses. Witnesses and coworkers develop a fear of their workplaces and lose confidence in anyone's ability to protect them. The person responsible for the violence most likely crumbled emotionally under the burden of stress he or she was carrying. Whether that stress is work related or due to some other factor, there are always signs that it could lead to an explosion of some kind.

For the company, violence affects how people function and how they feel about their jobs. Managers are often unprepared for and untrained in how to deal with such matters, leaving them guilt-ridden and confused after the fact. When employees and management are profoundly affected, everything suffers—productivity, morale, health, and a sense of security.

Many of the current approaches to workplace violence are clearly inadequate. The whole area of prevention consists of drafting hiring and firing policies, planning improved methods of security, and creating a profile of a "potentially violent employee." Response *after* the event is often too little, too late.

The key to dealing with violence in the workplace is the kind of prevention that includes the following:

- People at all levels are made aware of and educated about the potential for violent episodes.

- All employees are trained in how to settle disputes, improve communication, and negotiate areas of disagreement.

- The company has a crisis plan in place that is communicated, practiced, and implemented when necessary.

- Managers receive training in how to identify volatile employee situations with the potential for violence.

- Downsizings, layoffs, and terminations are handled thoughtfully, compassionately, and humanely.

- Clear rules for behavior as they relate to harassment, threats, abuse, disruption, and violent behavior are communicated and uniformly enforced.

Conclusion

It would be difficult to find a family to whom the word *dysfunctional* could not be applied, because there is no such thing as a perfect family. By the same token, you would be hard pressed to find a perfect organization, though there are some that could definitely be described as "excellent." If you work for one of those, you can consider yourself fortunate. If, on the other hand, as you read the list of "symptoms," you felt a sinking sensation in your stomach, your company probably would do well to take a self-inventory.

One way to help it do so is to pass along that list to the human resources department, your immediate supervisor, or someone you know, as high up in the organization as you can go. If you can encourage *even one person* with influence to ask how many of those symptoms apply to your organization and then be willing to do something about it, you will have made a significant contribution.

"Rome wasn't built in a day" means that things that are worth doing take time. One begins by identifying the problem, making a commitment to solve it, learning what it takes to do so, and taking that first step. Then it's a matter of putting one foot in front of the other, one day at a time.

CHAPTER EIGHT

Working in a Hierarchical Environment

John Burgess manages a staff of seventy-three people for a large aerospace company. He has an undergraduate degree in mechanical engineering and a graduate degree in engineering management. He joined his company fourteen years ago, right out of college, and financed his graduate degree with its educational reimbursement policy. He describes himself as "a classic middle manager," but one who traveled an atypical path to get to his present position. His company practices a hierarchical management style, but there is a positive side to that in this type of business, according to John Burgess.

Since I've been with the company, I have been through two levels of management. I was a group manager before this position and had ten people reporting to me. Now I have five group managers and their direct reports, so I am well aware of the kinds of issues they are dealing with. My group acts as a supplier of capital equipment for production. We determine what physical assets, resources, and processes production will be needed to do its job. We write the technical specifications for new equipment; negotiate the technical elements of the contract; act as project managers throughout acquisition; and, finally, release it to production.

This company is organized like a pyramid. At the top is the board of directors and the chairman of the board. Moving down, there is the CEO, president and chief operating officer, division presidents, executive vice-presidents, vice-presidents, division directors, directors, second-tier managers (which is my level), group managers, and the technical ranks. There are technical equivalents of those managerial positions all the way through the director level. The people who work on the line are all union. You can't transport or do manufacturing work on an airplane without belonging to the union.

I was hired into the product engineering organization as an associate engineer, and I did product design work for a few years. As I was designing structural parts, I decided I was going to learn a little bit more about how the airplane was built so that I could become a better designer in the long term. But in the short term, I needed to know how what I was designing was going to be fabricated. I wrote those kinds of things into my annual reviews and somebody noticed. I was put on to a rotation program through the manufacturing areas so that I got to work for a short time in many of the departments that support manufacturing.

It was an uncommon practice. It would have been more typical for me to join product engineering and rarely step out onto the manufacturing floor. Within the product engineering organization, I would put in some time as a design engineer on the boards. If I did a good job on that, I would become a lead man—someone who would know what to do next and essentially dole out assignments to his peers. If I did a good job there, I might be given a leadership role, either within a product-focused organization or in an engineering function. I could go up three or four levels that way.

While our management style is hierarchical, much of it has more to do with the personality of the person you are reporting to than to the corporate culture. I have had managers who weren't interested in knowing everything I did and who didn't mind if I dealt directly with their boss, if that is what is necessary to get the job done. I'd like to think that I am that kind of manager.

More dictatorial managers say, "You do not go around me." They become information bottlenecks and risk ending up with an organization that can only accomplish one thing at a time. I would much rather have my organization fighting the battle on many parallel fronts than waiting unnecessarily for my eyes to see everything that goes through.

The question really is whether one believes that a hierarchical structure adds or subtracts value from accomplishing the goal. I walked into my first managerial position thinking that this kind of structure would be an obstacle. I have softened on that point. I have begun to see that, when managers are skillful at working within such a system, they can add value by helping the organization run in the right direction and keeping what would otherwise be somewhat disconnected initiatives connected and integrated.

It is true that a hierarchy does have a tendency to slow things down, like running through mud. But I think a good manager finds a balance between two extremes. On one hand, you want to add value, integrate, and lead a group of people toward a vision. On the other hand, you don't want to make every project they pursue a serial exercise.

The opposite of a hierarchical organization is a *pancake* structure. A flatter structure is more entrepreneurial, more casual; but, in that environment, if I have a great idea, who do I tell? What steps do I go to through to get resources and a budget to pursue it? How do I even obtain authorization? At least, in my hierarchy, even though the process may be painfully slow, it is very clear what steps I have to go through.

It's important to remember the product we put together. We are not trying to penetrate some market niche somewhere. The things we build have a million fasteners and 250,000 parts, every one of which has to be to specification. This is not accomplished by a team of ten people. By the nature of the product, it takes *tens of thousands* of people in perhaps a hundred different disciplines to create it.

Remarkably, we do keep track of all the parts and processes. The product engineering organization says, "This is the intent of the design, and this is what the parts must look like." It maintains a configuration control of the parts; the metallurgy, chemistry, and process requirements; and how the product should be assembled. It is critical that we know the configuration of every ship that leaves here.

Then we have a quality organization that reports up through a completely different chain. It is their responsibility to audit that plane and the processes used in its fabrication and assembly process. The production group's charge is to muster resources to actually do the assembly work, which is being monitored every step of the way by these other two groups. Everyone has his own area of responsibility, and there is a hierarchy within each of three groups to ensure that it is all happening just as it should.

The best way to survive in this kind of management structure is to remain flexible, to understand what kind of people you are dealing with and what motivates them—particularly those above you in the hierarchy. What type of people are they? What synergy exists between your objectives and theirs? How long is your leash? If you have a short leash, and you expect to move up in the company, then you probably should find a way to be productive with a short leash.

If you find yourself in the opposite situation, you would do well to run as long as your leash will let you go. I think you will add more value to the organization if you play by those rules. Many free spirits are not team players. They make enemies, speak out in meetings when they shouldn't, and burn bridges.

Even in a hierarchical organization, it *is* possible to disagree with your boss, if he is open to discussion. My boss is well aware that, even if we disagree, at the end of the day *he is still the boss; and we do it his way.* The most important thing in an argument is to be sure that both parties are willing to change their positions given a good enough case. The best-case scenario is to be able to close the door, have the discussion, and leave with no hard feelings.

*   *   *

Some years ago a book appeared on the market that promised to show women *how to make it in the male-dominated business world.* The book was based on three ideas: the first, that business was a game—a game with an uneven playing field; the second, that women were at a disadvantage because they didn't know the rules; and, the third, that they didn't know the rules because they had never been in the military or played such team sports as football or soccer. Men, on the other hand, had done both; and, since business is organized much like the Army and played as a team sport, the book proposed to fill in these serious gaps in women's business education.

That book has long since become a collector's item for a number of reasons. Since it was published, women have been admitted in increasing numbers to West Point, Annapolis, and other formerly male bastions; they are not only *in* the military but rising to the highest ranks; and the popularity of women athletes and women's team sports is growing every day. More and more women are "making it" in the business world and, while it is still male dominated, more than a few are breaking through the proverbial glass ceiling.

One of the book's premises does remain intact, however. While U.S. businesses continue to downsize, flatten, and sweep middle managers out the door, most large corporations are still structured on the military model—an inverted pyramid, with the generals making decisions at the top and the foot soldiers carrying them out at the base. Much of America's workforce is employed in such companies. Whether you have been in the Army or played football, or never done either, if you work in that kind of environment, you must be able to function within a hierarchical structure.

The Top-Down System

What exactly does a hierarchical, top-down organization look like? For one thing, it is pretty much shaped like an upside down triangle. As in John Burgess's company, it usually has a president and CEO at the top. Reporting to that person are vice-presidents of various functions, and reporting to each of them are directors of departments within each function. Each director presumably oversees the work of several managers who, in turn, supervise work groups made up of various numbers of employees. At each level there are more people, with the employee base being the most heavily populated. Top-down cultures share a number of characteristics.

- Decisions are made at the top and either announced to the entire company or conveyed down through each level of the organization by various means—some effective, some not so effective. When information goes from one level to the next, like the children's game of telephone, it may change shape along the way. For one thing, what people receive depends to a great extent on how they interpret the information. Then, they pass their interpretation down the line. Second, they may not pass *all* of it along but only what they feel is necessary for the next level to know. So, the information becomes abbreviated or incomplete. And, third, how accurately the information is received hinges on how effectively it was sent and the recipients' interpretation of what they heard. If, by the end of the cycling-down process, the announcement of the decision in any way resembles the original version, it is close to a miracle.

• Change is slow, infrequent, and initiated at the top. In a top-down organization, if change is going to occur, it is rarely a grass-roots effort. The president, or the president and his or her executive management team, arrives at a policy decision and passes it along for implementation. Like decisions, the policy can become mangled in the communication process. Even if there is a general announcement, unless it is explained and people have an opportunity to respond to it and ask questions, the lower down on the pyramid one goes, the murkier the policy will be. In a hierarchical setup, sweeping change is rare because bringing it to fruition is a lot like reversing the way the earth revolves.

• Feedback and communication originate at the top, just as everything else does. Each level of management holds performance appraisals or their equivalent and informs the next level of how well they are doing. Rarely is there an opportunity for people to give feedback to their bosses on how well *they* are doing. Communication is initiated by management, who controls both the message and the medium. The only other ways information gets around is through "leaks," the rumor mill, or the ever-present grapevine.

• Managers tell employees what is expected of them, what to do, and sometimes how to do it. In this kind of arrangement, employees naturally focus upward to their immediate supervisors or managers for assignments, instructions, approval or disapproval, and rewards, which usually come in the form of promotions or pay raises. Initiative or creativity is neither expected nor encouraged.

• Employees are responsible for their own jobs and nothing else. When employees are empowered, they are responsible not only for doing their own jobs but for taking ownership of those jobs and seeking more efficient ways of performing them. When employees are empowered they represent the company to any outsider. They are ambassadors and problems solvers. If a caller or visitor has a problem, they either solve it personally or find a solution and get back to the person with the resolution. In a top-down environment, employees often pass people along from one department to another, in an attempt to get them off the phone or avoid responsibility for something that is *not their job.* They do not represent the company because they have never been asked or permitted to do so.

• There is tight control over employees' behavior. Top-down companies are hardly prisons, but they can feel like one. Whether it is due to management or a deeply ingrained corporate culture, there is a right way to act and a wrong way, a right way to dress and a wrong way. There is a well established protocol for everything, and often that protocol is wrapped in red tape. Employees of this kind of company have a certain look and a certain behavior. They are not hard to identify. Perhaps the best known example of this phenomenon was the "IBM Look" before the dress code loosened up. New employees caught on quickly and slipped almost unconsciously into *the look.* Rarely was it questioned; never was it ignored.

• In the midst of this environment—where decisions, information, communication, feedback, control, and rewards all come from the top, bestowed on the lower levels by an autocratic or benevolent management—employees are expected to be highly motivated. For a long time that expectation was met. People were motivated by extrinsic rewards to do their best. But, as quality-of-work-life issues and the desire to be heard and respected as people and contributors became more important to American workers, it took more than a corner office, a bonus, or a favorable contract to truly motivate people.

A Historical View

This may sound like "bad management" in light of today's new, more participatory philosophy; but remember that, for many years, this approach worked very effectively and in some companies still does. While not all corporations have changed their structure, the country has moved to a new paradigm of what constitutes good management.

In the past, there was an informal contract between management and employees that promised: *We'll take care of you if you work hard and are loyal to us.* Companies were like huge families run from the top by patriarchal, often paternal, leaders. Many people grew up in one company, retired with a gold watch, and saw their children coming right along behind them.

Hierarchical organizations were not only the norm, they were held in high esteem. People viewed them as structured, stable, and secure places to work. Those who found good jobs in them felt fortunate to be able to settle down for the long haul. In a way, they simply handed over responsibility for their daily activities, well-being, and future security to their employers, who gladly accepted the burden.

National pride was high; the economy was a reflection on the country's economic health. Business was—at the top levels, at least—pretty much a white, male-dominated world, which greatly influenced the corporate cultures. Education was a private affair, expected be completed before joining the company or on one's own time. People routinely started at the bottom and worked their way up in a step-by-step, linear career path. Each new position along the way had a title that was as definitive as wearing a label. When someone achieved a certain level and the corresponding title, everyone, including that person, knew exactly what status had been achieved.

All jobs had clear duties, with accountability to the next level of management. While there were few incentives or rewards, employees were expected to work hard and remain loyal to their employers. Most companies manufactured something and focused their attention on two things: selling their products and making money. Manufacturing companies were labor intensive; workers were often viewed more as tools than people. Quality control was not a household word; small errors were overlooked; and *close* was usually good enough.

A Whole New Ballgame

Contrast those values with what is in favor these days. It's no secret that the social contract has been broken beyond repair, and the idea of job security leading to a gold watch is a distant dream, or nightmare, depending on your viewpoint. Today's byword is *change. To* survive, one must be agile and flexible. Security means having portable skills and a high tolerance for living in limbo.

Finding a good job is still worth a celebration, but today's workers don't think much about settling down. With change occurring on every front, you—as one of them—have to stay aware and prepared. It is *your* responsibility, not your employer's, to provide for your own well-being, now and in the future. No one is going to do it for you.

The importance of positions and titles has been supplanted by the importance of having the skills and knowledge to do the job. Careers can rarely be described as linear. They are all over the place, sometimes moving sideways, sometimes in entirely new fields, and more and more often straight out of the corporate world. Entrepreneurial ventures are springing up every day; and, inside corporations, the same philosophy is at work in the form of *intrepreneurship.*

Don't worry about getting stuck in a rut. More than likely, you will have numerous and diverse duties that will require continuing education, cross training, and your active participation in the learning process. Knowledge is king, and employees are now viewed and valued as resources rather than as tools.

Outside forces are having a profound effect on today's workplace, both externally and internally. As more and more companies do business in other countries or have divisions abroad, the economy has shifted from a national focus to a global one. On every level people must learn to understand and work with those of other cultures. Internally, this same dynamic is taking place. The workplace is becoming much more diverse as women, people with disabilities, senior citizens, and those from many ethnic and cultural backgrounds give new meaning to the word diversity.

Education and work, unlike in the past, are interrelated and ongoing. Learning is expected to continue during one's whole life; many companies assist employees in going back to school or taking outside training; and the trend toward "learning organizations" is finding many new advocates.

One of the biggest changes is the switch from a manufacturing society to an information society. The product is not always tangible. Sometimes it isn't even a product. While keeping an eye on the bottom line is still very important, meeting the customers' needs, adding value to transactions, and providing knock-your-socks-off service have attained new stature. Another newly dusted-off concept is that of *quality.* Total Quality Management (TQM), ISO certification, and zero defects are becoming the rallying cry for U.S. business faced with international competition. In some plants, line workers are empowered to stop the line when they see a mistake. Close is not good enough any more; *perfect* is the goal.

Sounds like a different world, doesn't it? But, in fact, these new attitudes are being applied in many traditional, hierarchical businesses; and, in many cases, *they are working.* The point is that we should not write off the inverted pyramid completely. As John Burgess observed, organizations that have been flattened into pancakes have a host of drawbacks all their own. It isn't the way a company is organized that is the problem; it is obsolete attitudes that cannot work in today's global business environment.

Making the Transition

While the concepts of employee involvement and empowerment are hardly new, they take time to catch on and to filter through hierarchical organizations. In addition to time, a successful transition from *the old way* to *the new way* depends on a number of other important elements:

- buy-in and commitment on the part of senior management
- a program to help management and employees cope with change
- company-wide systems to bring the new philosophy to life and make it relevant in the real world
- an ongoing, well planned, and well executed communication strategy
- incentives to keep the program alive and employees involved
- feedback and evaluation at every step of the process
- follow-up training and communications to ensure that the new way becomes an integral part of the corporate culture

Obviously, this is a tall order and something no company should attempt without a great deal of thought and discussion. While empowering employees and having them participate in solving problems, redesigning their jobs, and becoming part of self-managing teams may *seem* like a tremendous improvement over top-down management, it can backfire. Many companies that have tried to institute participative management and employee involvement have found, to their dismay, that not everyone wanted to participate or to be involved.

In fact, many employees were much more comfortable being told what to do and how and when to do it. Taking responsibility for their jobs, their decisions, and their individual contributions was overwhelming and threatening to them. Empowerment was not only unwelcome, it often met with tremendous resistance. The new paradigm may indeed be a better way to run a company and maximize the contributions of its people, but not everyone can handle change or wants to be empowered.

If you do work for such a company, the question on your mind may be, *How can I survive and thrive in this environment?* There are two guidelines that can help you do both. As John noted, much of your ability to function in a hierarchical organization has more to do with the personality of your immediate manager than with the corporate culture. Thus, the first guideline is to evaluate your boss's style, to find areas of flexibility, and to make the most of them. In other words, *learn to manage your boss.*

The second guideline assumes that, even if you were in a maximum security prison, you would always have a little room in which to maneuver. A former convict insists that, if you know the *size of the playing field* (the rules and boundaries) and remain inside the lines, you have the freedom to do more than you would dream. Just don't step over the edge.

An even more dramatic demonstration of this concept comes from Viktor Frankl, the famous psychiatrist and author of *Man's Search for Meaning.* Frankl, who survived internment in a concentration camp, postulated that the smallest playing field in the world is *one's own mind,* in which one has total freedom to think, respond, and interpret life as one wishes. The second guideline, then, is know the size of your playing field—the boundaries within which you can play— and then design your own game. In other words, *empower yourself.*

In Section Three of this book, an entire chapter is devoted to managing your boss, but here is a sneak preview to give you a head start on the first guideline.

- Try to understand your boss's feelings, pressures, and needs.
- Know what causes him stress. If you understand his stressors, you will be in a better position to help minimize them.
- Know that your boss needs people she can trust, who do their jobs well, who are good communicators, who run interference when necessary, and who understand the demands of her job. Be one of those people.
- When your boss tells you something, don't repeat it. If he makes a mistake and you know about it, make sure no one else knows about it.
- When you say you will do something or be somewhere, do it or be there.
- Show up for work every day; know your job; do your job.
- Be present in mind as well as body.
- Don't ever undermine your boss; protect her professional image and reputation.
- Know your boss's day-to-day responsibilities; her relationship with *her* boss; and what it takes to do her job.

If you have a job, you fit *somewhere* in the hierarchy of your organization. Whatever your level, you are accountable to someone up the line, especially in a top-down company. Precisely *because* you work in that kind of corporate culture, you may often feel a lack of control over the circumstances that shape your daily activities. Perhaps everything from your boss's management style to the normal constraints of a hierarchical culture are contributing to your prevailing feeling of powerlessness, frustration, and stress.

The truth is you have more *power,* or control, than you realize. You have control over your attitudes, the goals you set, the choices you make, and the degree to which you involve yourself in your job. Let us assume that you are *not* one of those people who will run screaming in the other direction at the sound of the word *empowerment;* that you have assessed the size and scope of your playing field; and that you know you can work within its boundaries. Now what?

First you must realize that no one can empower you but you. Personal power is an innate quality. It is only necessary to recognize and tap into what is already there. Self-empowerment is, by definition, an individual responsibility. In an empowering environment—even if that is only your own little department, in the midst of a sea of autocracy—you must know what to do with authority when it is given to you. You must learn how to use it for the benefit of the organization and for your own growth. The point is, *if you stay inside your playing field, you have many* options and opportunities to make your own choices and write your own job description.

Here are 14 things you can do to empower yourself right now:

1. *Be a well-rounded individual.* Seek balance in your life, and don't fall into the workaholic trap.

2. *Analyze your boss's skills.* Ask yourself how your own strengths fill the gaps where she has weaknesses. Observe people who have been promoted. What did they do? Where did they excel?

3. *Be results-oriented.* Focus on the things you can control, and work to get things done. Don't waste your energy on frustration about things you can't control.

4. *Become a generalist.* Specialization is out. Don't allow yourself to be stuck in a narrow niche. The broader your skills are, the more marketable you will be.

5. *Build coalitions, teams, and collaborative, not competitive, relationships.* *Sell* (rather than *tell)* your ideas to others. Become a team player.

6. *Create a job for yourself.* Don't wait to be slotted in the formal structure. Identify something important that needs to be done, and demonstrate how you can do it.

7. *Devise an intermediate-term and a long-term strategy.* What skills do you need to develop to improve your performance in the job you have and in the job you want? Take courses to gain or improve those skills. Ask for assignments that will help you develop them.

8. *Establish and build your credibility.* Think like a businessperson. Study the issues. Identify problems, and propose viable solutions. Take some risks.

9. *Market yourself internally.* Let others know who you are, what you know, what interests you, and what you can do. Spread the word that you're available for jobs or assignments that open up.

10. *Learn how things get done in your company.* Identify those managers who are really influential. Get yourself known and hooked into the informal information channels.

11. *Look at supply and demand in your job category.* If there's an oversupply, consider shifting career paths. This is not an easy piece of advice to accept, especially if you have spent a lot of time getting to where you are at this moment.

12. *Tune into your environment.* Be aware of everything that goes on around you. Develop the ability to look at existing processes, spin them around, and put them into a different context.

13. *Question routine procedures, and devise other ways to do them.* Visualize a new way of doing things, the outcomes, and results. Communicate those ideas to others.

14. *Request more accountability and responsibility,* rather than more money. Pick up any slack you see by taking on more work. Accepting accountability and responsibility are pivotal aspects of self-empowerment.

Conclusion

Philosophies and styles of management come and go. What was acceptable in the fifties is passé in the eighties and all but forgotten in the nineties. Theory Z, quality circles, accelerated learning, and "thriving on chaos" are all ideas that captured imaginations and spurred great activity, only to be replaced by newer, supposedly better, more up-to-date philosophies that may be obsolete tomorrow.

The way companies are organized, the way they manage, the way they achieve and measure success are distinct—company to company, decade to decade, and management expert to management expert. Some things, of course, appear to be gone for good. Among them are total disregard for employees as human beings; the thirty-year career in one place; perhaps the gold watch and guaranteed pension; and, most certainly, mimeograph machines, typewriters, and carbon copies.

One thing that is not gone, and may refuse to leave in the foreseeable future, is the hierarchical organizational structure, whether or not it works and whether it is in favor or out. Since it seems to be here for the short term, you would do well to develop a strategy to flourish in this environment.

CHAPTER NINE

Seeing Through the Myth of Invincibility

Lou Kalosc *is director of financial communications for a* Fortune *500 company located in the Midwest. He began his career as a newspaper reporter and made what he calls "the natural transition" into public relations. A* nice guy, *who practices the Golden Rule in all aspects of his life, he learned the hard way that, when you work for a company that thinks it's invincible, that rule no longer applies.*

I worked for an international communications agency based in Minneapolis. It had offices in several other cities and countries, as well as affiliates all over the world. There were some pretty high expectations going into this job. I had been in the newspaper business for a major metropolitan daily for eight years, so I had a strong writing background. When I joined the agency, it was just entering its major growth phase.

The company knew what it would take to be the best. One of the things they told me at my interview was, *If you want to be a family man and be home to play with your kids every night, this isn't the place to work. But if you want to be able to put your kids through Ivy League schools, this is where you want to be.* They were telling me my family wasn't important to them and that the most important thing in *my* life must be the agency. I took the job, but I knew I wouldn't be there long.

It was an era of *we can do no wrong,* and I found it strange to be associated with a company that really believed it was infallible. The pressure was on to live up to those standards. As I found, after I'd been there a while, there was a *lot* they actually did do wrong; but they just swept it aside, saying, in effect, *We are who we are.* They never admitted they had made a mistake, but in public relations there is a way to twist things so that people actually believe whatever you tell them. There were a few instances where they made *big* mistakes, but somehow they managed to talk their way out of them.

In my heart I knew that some of the things that were going on around me were wrong; and, at the same time, I was hearing how they were being explained. I knew people could believe that. I think, eventually, even *I* could have begun to believe it. So, there was a struggle going on in me. Ethically, I was asking, *Is what we're doing the right thing?* And the answer I was getting was, *We are the best. We represent the greatest companies in the world. There is a reason why we've achieved this status, why we are this big and this great.*

They believed their own propaganda. It got to the point where, if someone in the media crossed them, they could say to that person, *This is what you're going to have to do to pay for your mistake, if you ever want a story from us again.* They often got away with that, but some members of the press said, *Forget it! We don't need you. We'll circumvent you every chance we get.* In return, the agency cut them off. Because they have such great relationships with their clients, they had complete control of the flow of information.

I've been on both sides of that fence. As a reporter, if you wrote proactive, positive articles about some of the things the agency was trying to promote, you were in really good with them and could always get information. The first time you crossed them, though, you were out. I've seen it happen. They don't return phone calls; they ignore deadlines; they hold back information. It is an abuse of power. When you work there, you sense that power. When I crossed over from media to the agency, the media couldn't stand who I had become.

That put me in an awkward position because I still had a lot of friends in the media. One of the reasons I was hired in the first place was because I had that kind of access. I had built solid relationships that would work in the agency's favor as I began to pitch stories on behalf of my clients. Because the media got so little information from us, when we did call with something, they thought it must be important. That's why a lot of what we pitched was fairly well received. They felt if this agency was involved, it must be legit.

I was never one to be really impressed with myself. I pride myself on the relationships I've built, and I work hard to maintain those relationships. I didn't take my friends to lunch or try to buy their friendship. I did stay in touch—called every now and then just to shoot the breeze about old times. We'd go out for a beer, not to try to influence them, but to maintain the relationship. I took the job because it was a good opportunity and a way to make some good contacts, but I didn't plan to stay there longer than five years. I didn't even last that long.

There were a lot of internal politics. I was on a team that had fourteen members. There were divisions within our team and a lot of pulling and pushing in one direction or another. Instead of working together as a team, people would walk over a teammate to get what they wanted. I had a hard time playing that game. In fact, that was the biggest reason behind my decision to leave. I couldn't deal with that divisiveness on my own team.

Another reason was the issue of fair recognition. There were stories I set up and pitched that other people tried to take credit for. They were people who knew how to play the game and didn't care about who they offended or who they walked over. Because they had been there longer than I had and had better connections to higher-level executives, *they* were recognized for things *I* had done. I tried to fight for what I felt I deserved, but I was perceived as a malcontent or somebody who was trying to stir the pot. When you're in that environment, if you can't get credit for your achievements, what's the point?

The agency's goal was to be the biggest and the best—number one. They worked hard to achieve top status and built relationships with influencers in the media to help them do it. Those people thought the agency could do no wrong and, since the agency believed that too, that's the way we all lived. There was always pressure to win, even when we were supposed be having fun.

We were a closed, insulated society. Spouses were never invited to company functions. It was almost as if they didn't exist. The danger of working for a company that thinks it's invincible is that you begin to believe you can do anything, that you can get away with anything. This attitude carries over to the way you live. You think, *Hey, I work for this agency. We're number one, and no one can touch us. Therefore, I'm special because I'm part of this group.* No wonder people thought we were arrogant.

The perception out there is that the agency is the Holy Grail. If you work for them, you can pick your next job. You can write your own ticket. People who have a chance to go to work for them come to me for advice. I tell them, *If you go there, you'd better be prepared not to have a life. If you have family, tell your wife she'll be playing second fiddle to your job. Above all, don't let them kill your integrity.*

When I see my friends who still work there, they can't look me in the eye. It's almost as of they are ashamed of what they do. I've been in their position. I know too much. If I had stayed, I would have felt the same way—embarrassed—even though *We were number one.*

*   *   *

If you have ever met someone with what we used to call "a superiority complex," you know how self-righteous and arrogant such people can be. They can do no wrong; they know all the answers; their behavior seems to say, "My way or the highway." Today, we might use words like egotistical or narcissistic to describe them; but the personality traits would be much the same. These people don't listen. They already know the answers, and they don't want to be confused with facts. They are always right and often see themselves as indestructible. They are also hard to take.

Organizations can have the same "personality," and, when they do, they are equally hard to take. If you work in one, you know that your relationship with your employer is more complicated than it would be with an overconfident friend. You could conceivably leave your friend; leaving your place of employment is not so easy.

This chapter explores the myth of invincibility such companies perpetuate, the signs to look for, and the repercussions of this myth.

Maintaining the Myth

As we can see from Lou Kalosc's story, the consequences of a company accepting its own image of invincibility can be very serious. People's feelings are disregarded; integrity and honesty are sacrificed; major mistakes are made and then covered up; impossible standards are set; dissent is not tolerated; and employees play by the rules or get out of the game.

Examples of such major mistakes are legendary: Companies misjudge their markets and end up in bankruptcy; governments pursue flawed foreign policies and find themselves on the brink of war; federal agencies approve drugs that have unimagined side effects or authorize "perfectly safe" chemicals that turn out to be poisonous; utilities erect nuclear power plants to generate power cheaply and safely, only to end up charging consumers for their costly and sometimes dangerous miscalculations.

How and why do such errors occur? Isn't anyone inside or outside the company policing the operation? What's the problem here? The problem is often plain, old human error. People make mistakes; and, if adequate quality controls and checks and balances are not in place, those mistakes slip through, sometimes with dire consequences. Decisions are made based on emotion, insufficient information, simplistic thinking, refusal to dig for the truth, and personal prejudices.

Decisions are also often made by groups. Some groups sabotage themselves because of bad leadership or worse processes. Groups, at their worst, sometimes assume almost a mob mentality that can lead to results ranging from mindless conformity to panic and violence. Groups are subject to complacency, glossing over information that doesn't fit their model, and excessive risk taking. Groups also have a tendency to develop negative stereotypes of anyone considered an outsider.

Group leaders may bully, persuade, cajole, or find other ways of imposing their views on the members. Group leaders can ignore input and feedback and insist on a rubber stamp for their decisions, or, at the other extreme, passively give in to the desires of the group, ignoring their own instincts.

Group members may force their views on each other, exert subtle or not-so-subtle constraints on speaking up or disagreeing, and squelch critical thinking and dissent. They can compete rather than collaborate; pursue private agendas rather than group goals; and, as we have seen, "walk all over people to get what they want." On the other hand, group members can agree on everything and be so cohesive that no one thinks to question their collective conclusions. Such group cohesiveness can be dangerous to the organization's health because it leads to mindless conformity and slipshod thinking.

Serious Symptoms

How do you know if you work for a company that views itself as invincible? Here are some red flags.

Denial

Denial is when people don't admit what is really happening. If management refuses to face facts or closes its eyes to unwanted information, it is lying to itself, its employees, and all others who have a stake in the company. An entire organization can be in denial when it just won't acknowledge what is going on within its walls or outside in its markets. This kind of denial takes many forms.

Companies deny the negative effects of their products on consumers and on the environment. Management complies with OSHA safety requirements only as far as it must to keep from being fined. Employees close their eyes to unethical behavior, addiction, and bullying. Everyone denies there is prejudice, discrimination, and inequality in the workplace.

Denial is like a virulent virus. It spreads until the entire company is sick. It may start small with ignoring the actions of a destructive or addicted supervisor, but eventually it will spread to other people and processes until it becomes a way of life. Denial leads to dishonesty. It prevents people from speaking their minds, calling attention to the obvious, and questioning what should be questioned. It encourages secrecy and withholding of information, covering up one's mistakes, and outright lying. After a while, this way of doing things becomes so natural that no one questions it. It is simply "the way things are."

Isolation and Insulation

Invincible companies, like invincible people, have a rather exaggerated view of their importance. They tend to see themselves as the center of the universe and the holder of all the really important information. It is not enough for them to deny internally whatever is actually happening; it is important to keep outsiders from knowing as well. A second characteristic of invincibility is isolation from outside influences. It is also a very good way to stay far from customers, clients, communities, and everyone else. This is particularly true of nonprofit service organizations, many of which have developed the ability to have virtually no contact with the clients they serve. Isolation leads to insulation and secrecy. Company secrets don't get out, and unwanted information doesn't get in. Whatever illusion the company has created, it remains intact because there is nothing and no one to dispel it.

Personalization and Judgment

To be judgmental means to be critical, to label things as good or bad—most often bad. Invincible companies make these sort of judgments. Behavior, achievement, or lack of it are used to measure the worth of a person. If an employee is falling short, it isn't the *work* that is criticized; it is the *person* who is found wanting. This creates a kind of paranoia about stepping out of line or failing in some way, with the inevitable consequence being judgment. Judgmental companies prevent growth, limit creativity, encourage dishonesty, put people on the defensive, and perpetuate the status quo.

Perfectionism

Invincible companies have delusions of grandeur. Like Lou Kalosc's agency, they can accomplish everything, get away with anything, and exert control over anyone. In short, they think they are perfect; and that is the standard they expect everyone to meet. Perfectionism is an illusion, and the only way to maintain it is to close one's eyes to reality. A company that refuses to see imperfection, does not tolerate it, and lies to cover it up has bought into the illusion and is in serious denial.

This is evidenced by its corporate mission statements, company-wide strategic objectives and even job descriptions. If no human being could ever hope to achieve the objectives laid out in his or her job description, that's a clue. Service organizations that have grandiose visions, like feeding every starving child in the world, have set up an impossible goal. But goals keep everyone looking toward the future instead at what is going on right this minute. Perfection is always possible in the somewhere out there.

Crisis Mentality

A crisis is disruptive and distracting. If one is occurring, all hands must be on deck to deal with it. The very life of the organization, it would seem, depends on putting out this fire, right now. A crisis unites adversaries by giving everyone a shared mission—to work together for the common good. It creates a sense of camaraderie and teamwork in what is often a competitive environment. A crisis provides an opportunity for the expression of emotions—approved, sanctioned emotions that focus on the company, not on the individual. A crisis reinforces the notion that the situation can be resolved if enough control is exercised, that together we can do anything. A crisis covers up a lot of mistakes by diverting attention from them. When crisis is more usual than unusual, it gives top management a great deal of power.

Seduction

Anne Wilson Schaef and Diane Fassel, authors of *The Addictive Organization,* define seduction as "a process of luring people away from their own perceptions and their knowing what is right for them.""In such organizations," they write, "people often find themselves getting on bandwagons or being pulled into activities that do not feel right to them." That was certainly Lou's experience when he asked if what they were doing was *the right thing* and felt even he could eventually come to believe it was.

Manipulation

Since invincible organizations can do no wrong, they will do anything to perpetuate their agendas, whether that is lying, suppressing information, manipulating the media, or intimidating employees. The end justifies the means. It is important for everyone to be playing on the same team, to be singing out of the same hymnal. In many companies, if someone is not considered *a player,* that person is cut out of the loop, ostracized, or even fired. One strategy is to privately let others know that this is a *persona non grata* and it would be better for their careers to not be seen associating with him. This presents a terrible moral dilemma for people and is one of the ways in which they are manipulated into compromising their values to save their jobs.

"Groupthink"

Groupthink is a made-up word that has become part of the business vernacular, much like *Kleenex* and *Xerox* and *Scotch Tape*. Few of us remember that those are registered brand names, not generic words. Since Irving L. Janis wrote *Victims of Groupthink* in 1972, it has become impossible to describe his concept without using this word that so perfectly captures it.

"Groupthink," wrote Janis, "is a term that refers to a mode of thinking that people engage in when they are deeply involved in a cohesive in-group, when the members' striving for unanimity overrides their motivation to realistically appraise alternative courses of action ... Groupthink refers to a deterioration of mental efficiency, reality testing, and moral judgment that result from in-group pressures."

Symptoms of "Groupthink"

Groups that suffer from this malady look ideal at first glance, but their defects soon become apparent. They are characterized by:

- a shared illusion of invincibility, optimism, and willingness to take extreme risks
- the ability to rationalize decisions, ignore red flags, and refuse to examine assumptions
- an unquestioned belief in the morality of the group and its decisions
- stereotyping and blanket put-downs of those considered to be the enemy
- discouragement of dissent and direct pressure on anyone who expresses disagreement, objections, or opposing points of view

- self-censorship to prevent anyone from deviating from group consensus
- insistence on unanimous support for the majority view
- self-appointed mindguards who protect the group from information that might shatter its self-satisfaction

"My assumption is that the more frequently a group displays these symptoms, the worse will be the quality of its decisions," wrote Janis more than twenty-five years ago. "The more amiability and *esprit de corps* among the members of an in-group of policy makers, the greater is the danger that independent critical thinking will be replaced by Groupthink." Janis went on to support his theory by analyzing some of the worst fiascoes of our time, including the "surprise" bombing of Pearl Harbor, the Bay of Pigs Invasion, the Korean War, and the escalation of the war in Viet Nam—all dramatic consequences of Groupthink.

What all of those events have in common is that those involved in the decision-making process caved in to the apparent preferences of the group. When they should have raised objections, they remained silent. When they should have questioned the reliability of the intelligence at their disposal, they failed to do so. When opposing views were voiced, they were ignored or suppressed. When the smoke cleared, in some cases, those who had dissented were fired.

In each case the top teams felt strongly that they were making the best possible decisions and that there was unanimous agreement to proceed. They *knew* they were morally correct, they were united in their confidence in the plan, and they were insulated from outside feedback. In all cases, they were wrong. How could this have happened? Here are some possibilities:

- Only a few options were actually considered and discussed.

- Proposed solutions and courses of action that were favored early in the discussions were dismissed and never revisited.

- Once a course of action was labeled "unsatisfactory" by the majority, it died.

- Little or no attempt was made to obtain information from experts who could have assessed the value or drawbacks of the proposed solutions.

- The group, as a whole, tended to accept facts and outside opinions that supported its policies and to ignore those that did not.

- Decisions were made on shaky assumptions.

- There was little thought or air time given to how decisions or policies might be derailed or sabotaged.

- Since those things were not considered, there was no contingency plan in the event of failure.

The Myth of Invincibility

Myth is another word for illusion, and invincible organizations live in a world of illusions. One is that they are invulnerable. Nothing can hurt them. They are impervious to the repercussions and dangers that might follow from taking certain risks, especially if everyone thinks they should go for it. The group has great confidence in and admiration for the leader. If the leader supports taking the risk, the feeling is that it can't fail. Luck will be on their side.

As Lou observed, there is a sense of belonging to a powerful, protective group that can do just about anything. That makes all of the members special; and, even though no individual is a superman, the group is seen as a supergroup, capable of surmounting all obstacles. Not only can they do it, they can get away with it. They are the guys in the white hats, the good guys who will win in the end. Conversely, their opponents are the bad guys.

Another illusion is that of unanimity. The thinking is: *We all agree; we all believe this; therefore, it must be true. If we are unanimous, we don't have to test our hypothesis or think critically. If we all see it the same way, there is no reason to explore opinions that might disrupt our unity.* Lack of argument or silence is taken as consent. During the meeting that lead to the Bay of Pigs debacle during the Kennedy Administration, Secretary of State Dean Rusk said little and was presumed to be in agreement with the invasion plan. In fact, he was not.

Why didn't he speak up? Perhaps he was reluctant to raise questions that might cast doubt on a plan that appeared to have the approval of the rest of the group. Or maybe his misgivings didn't seem strong enough to warrant arguing against it and alienating everyone else.

"Self-appointed *mindguards*," wrote Janis, "protect leaders from thoughts that might damage their confidence in the soundness of the policy to which they are committed. When someone does have the courage to disagree and deviate from the dominant beliefs of the group, he or she is often urged to remain silent." A perfect example of this phenomenon took place when the president's brother reportedly said to one of the members of the group, "You may be right or you may be wrong, but the President has made his mind up. Don't push it any further."

Sometimes it is not the group that is reticent to rock the boat; it is the leader, who may resort to subtle pressures to maintain the status quo. That makes it very difficult to object, to suggest other approaches, or to raise critical issues. There is no question that any group agenda can be manipulated by a smooth, silver-tongued leader. Even if dissenting views are expressed, such a leader may provide no opportunity to explore or discuss them. By cutting them off at the pass, the leader is sending a clear message: *Drop it.*

Every executive who participates in group decisions runs the risk of succumbing to Groupthink. Within the larger group there is often a subgroup that subtly or not so subtly orchestrates the agenda and the outcome. The more insulated and cut off from outsiders such a group is, the greater the risk that its decisions will be a product of Groupthink. If the leader is strong enough or persuasive enough, he can easily generate the consensus he needs to support his position.

Conclusion

Organizations that truly believe they can do no wrong are no different than countries that operate on the premise of invulnerability. If management perpetuates this belief and convinces or coerces employees to accept it as well, they create toxic work environments. What do you do if you work for one?

First, of course, you must recognize the symptoms and determine just how sick your company is. Then, consider your options. You can accept it and adjust; fight it and risk losing; try to change the culture; or leave, as Lou Kalosc did. These are not easy choices. One must weigh security and family responsibilities against a noisy conscience and a sense of right and wrong.

In the best of all possible worlds you might be able to influence change or be free to simply walk away; but in the cold, clear light of day, either may be a very difficult thing to do. There are no simple answers to this question. Each person must make his or her own judgment call on what is certainly the horns of a dilemma.

CHAPTER TEN

Maneuvering Around the Obstacle Course

Kate Sullivan is a Minneapolis high school health and physical education teacher who jumps over hurdles, knocks them down, or goes around them if she has to. She has learned to negotiate workplace obstacle courses in retail, restaurant, and academic settings. In her present position, she does whatever it takes to give her students the best possible educational experience she can create for them.

I'm kind of a rebel. So, most of the things I want to do are things that have never been done before or that require manipulating, moving, or finding resources. This almost always causes complete upheaval. When I try to be innovative in a place where people have done things in exactly the same way for a very long time, it's inevitable that I will step on some toes; and I have.

Most of my prior experience was in the retail and restaurant industries. From the very beginning of my career, I've been client-centered. I have known who my clients or customers were and what it would take to meet their needs. In the school setting, my clients are the students, and I do whatever it takes to meet their needs. To accomplish that, I often have to deal with the administration—which isn't always on my wave length—because almost everything I do requires approval from someone at that level. I'm not very political, and I sometimes forget that I have to go through all the appropriate channels to get to the person whose approval I need.

When I first started teaching at this school, I just went straight to that person. It worked, but there were many people I bypassed on my way there. Frankly, I think that *is* the way to get things done, but I alienated some people at the bottom of the ladder by doing it that way. I've learned that eventually I *will* get to the person I need; but, in the long run, it's better to gain support along the way than it is to jump over everybody.

One of the biggest hurdles I encounter in my job is the unavailability of the facilities, resources, or equipment I need in order to teach. If I want to use them for something that's never been done before, I have to practically invent a way to get them. The problem is often that what I want to do conflicts with after-school activities—what is going on that evening or over the weekend.

The gym is the central location for activity—daytime, nighttime, all the time. Unfortunately, the daytime activities don't necessarily take precedence. If there's a basketball game that night, someone will invariably insist on hanging a sign up *right now.* Even though they've had that sign for four months, *today* is the day it has to be hung, in the middle of my volley-ball game. For three weeks, they were putting up new lights in the gym. There was scaffolding and apparatus all over the place, just sitting out in the middle of the gym floor. Two days in a row, electricians were installing a brand new stereo system on the ceiling, with kids playing all around them. Everyone is busy doing their own thing and using my classroom to do it.

When I want to do something, I'm a master at maneuver-ing. If I hit one obstacle, I tend to go a different route. If I want to plan a new program, I know what the steps are to get what I want. I ask a lot of questions and usually get around whomever or whatever is in my way.

When I first came here, I watched, I listened, and I talked to people who had been here a long time. I looked at things they were doing that I liked and found out what they had to do to make them happen. I have basically figured out who I need to know, who the right people are, who is in charge of what, who is going to be an advocate for the client, who is going to support my causes, who has the power, and who con-trols the purse strings. At my school, there are many different ways to get funding, and almost everything I want to do costs money.

I write grants. I find out who's in charge of the technolo-gy money. I research which clubs and student groups support what projects, go to their meetings, and find ways to get them to pay for things. I use all my resources. It was hard to find that information. In the beginning, I was just trying to figure out how to take attendance.

Some people don't go that extra mile or achieve what they could achieve because they hit one of these roadblocks early on. When they come up with a minor project and run into one hundred obstacles right away, they just give up. Consequently, they don't get the chance to do exciting, different things. Even taking a field trip is a hassle. You have to fill out forms. You have to organize the bus. The kids have to pay for the bus. Every single thing turns into a major ordeal.

There are so many different aspects to every activity—the school board, finances, the administration, parents, kids, and facilities, to name a few. If you're new and haven't had much experience at this sort of thing, you don't think about things from all those perspectives. You have tunnel vision; you just want to do what you want to do. I've learned to try to see my projects from all of those perspectives, to talk to peers about what others in the approval loop may be thinking. Then when I go to them for an O.K., I am able to articulate *their* perspective much more effectively than in the past. Before, I just charged ahead. I don't do that anymore.

A perfect example of the way I *used* to handle things is when I wanted my kids to roller skate. The first thing I did was call the superintendent of curriculum ... *at home.* He thought it was a great idea; but the more we got into it, the more people became involved. The principal had to approve it; the district superintendent had to know about it; the parents were interested; the school board got involved. It was a *one-week* deal that took months of pre-planning: writing letters, fighting with the basketball coach, getting access to the stereo system, having permission slips signed—all this for a one-week activity, where we were not even leaving campus.

The longer I do this, the more I take a deep breath at the beginning and say, *Here we go.* When I first got here, I didn't do that. I would get these wild ideas and just jump in, not realizing any of the ramifications. I've been going to meetings for two and a half years, learning about heart rate monitors. Last year everything clicked, and I decided we had to have them.

From the start, I thought, *What is this going to take?* I went through the steps, got permission to buy them, made a presentation to the school board, and was given the money. It was and still is a great project.

What keeps me going, what pushes me to continue to be innovative and to try to make it happen, is the reaction of my students. They are—in their own teenage way—appreciative and responsive. They know they're not getting the standard run-of-the-mill, throw-the-ball-out education. They understand what it took to get the program, whatever that program may be, approved and implemented. And they are grateful. That's enough for me.

*   *   *

One of the strangest things about working for a living is how difficult it sometimes seems simply *to do your job.* The strange part is not that you don't know what to do or how to do it or that you lack the skills, the desire, or the energy to do it. It is almost as if there were a silent conspiracy in place with only one aim: to make your life miserable and your job impossible. Of course, this makes no sense. Yet, this strange phenomenon is as inevitable and as prevalent as smoke-free buildings. The trick is to identify the specific obstacle that is impeding your progress and develop a strategy for getting past it, so that you can do what you are being paid to do. Here are a few real accounts of some of the more common hurdles you might encounter.

Paradoxical Priorities

Tracy got all her *firsts* out of the way in a single day. She encountered her *first* hurdle in the business world on the *first* day of her *first* real job. She was sixteen years old, a junior in high school, and full of energy when she landed a part-time job in a retail sporting goods store just before Christmas. It was the perfect job for an athletic, ambitious, and people-oriented teenager who was eager to earn some spending money.

She had spent her first Saturday morning unpacking cartons, hanging up parkas, and stocking shelves with ski sweaters. The afternoon looked like it was going to be more of the same. While it wasn't really very interesting, Tracy didn't mind doing it. It helped her learn the merchandise and was physical enough to pass for exercise. In fact, she was actually enjoying organizing the sweaters on each shelf in what she thought was a very eye-catching arrangement.

About two o'clock, she noticed a customer walking around with a pile of ski clothes in her arms and an exasperated look on her face. The store had been very busy most of the day but was completely empty at the moment, except for this customer and Tracy. Everyone else seemed to have disappeared. The woman was juggling the clothes in one arm and going through a pile of turtleneck shirts with the other. She kept dropping things and couldn't seem to find exactly what she was looking for. She was clearly frustrated.

She caught sight of Tracy and asked in a loud voice, "Can you help me?" Tracy left her half-empty carton and raced across the store. The customer was looking for a man's turtle neck in a particular color and size. When she managed to find the right color, it was in the wrong size; and when she found the right size, it wasn't the right color. She was also in a bit of a hurry, she told Tracy, and had been searching in vain for some time.

"Not a problem," Tracy assured her. "I'll just go look in the back. I'm sure we have it." She was very pleased with herself when she located the right color and size and brought it out. By this time, the customer was hunting for her charge plate, as the cashier began to ring up her pile of purchases. The customer left happy because she had found everything she wanted; the cashier who rang up the sale was happy because he worked on commission and this had been a sizable sale; and Tracy was happy because she felt she had handled the situation quite professionally. Is this the end of a success story? Not quite: The store manager, it seems, was not at all happy.

If Tracy expected a pat on the back, what she received instead was a frosty lecture on "abandoning her assignment." She was stunned by the criticism. What had she done wrong? "We have to get that merchandise out on the floor. That's *very* important," the manager told her. "You walked away and left a carton sitting in the middle of the floor ... sweaters here, there, and everywhere ... and three shelves with nothing on them!"

The three shelves seemed to be the problem, at least from her tone of voice; but Tracy couldn't be sure. As she opened her mouth to reply, the manager cut her off. "If you don't mind," she said icily, "would you finish what you started over there?" Then she walked away, leaving Tracy deflated and confused.

How could putting sweaters on shelves be more important than waiting on customers? The customer had *asked* for help. There was no one else around. What else could she have done? And wasn't the whole point of being a salesperson to *sell* things? Perhaps she had it all wrong. Apparently, it wasn't *selling* that mattered; it was making sure the shelves were full. That made no sense to her at all, but then she figured she had lots to learn about working.

And the Obstacle Is ...?

Inside-out priorities, procedures take precedence, no sense of why the store was in business, customer service at the bottom of the list, and poor management are just a few of the problems Tracy encountered here. She may have been young and inexperienced, but her instincts were correct: The first priority *is* to take care of the customer. While it seems inconceivable that the manager was merely following company policy by insisting that stock issues were more important than service issues, in reality, it is possible. Inattention to and disregard for service frequently do start at the top and filter down through a company.

But to be charitable, let us assume that there simply was no policy and that the store manager exercised her own value system. In her mind, finishing the job she had begun should have been Tracy's highest priority. The fact that there would be no reason to unload cartons and stock shelves if there were no customers never entered her mind. Sad to say, this kind of skewed approach to priorities is all too common in retail establishments. While the vignette doesn't tell us whether Tracy eventually blasted this particular obstacle out of her way, we can only hope that her sense of what was really important overcame this flawed reasoning eventually.

Classic Mismatch

Alec was a writer—a very good writer, in fact. He had spent the last seventeen years building a successful career, first in journalism and then in corporate communications. But, if the truth be known, he hated his job. He was doing all the writing, photography, and art direction for three different publications; traveling three weeks out of four; and working in what he considered a crazy house. His salary was not what it should have been at this stage of his life, and he couldn't see anywhere to go in this company. He felt stuck.

That's why he was so tempted by the possibility of going to work for the consulting firm he had met with again today. Three interviews into the process, he was getting the idea he was the front-runner. The money was much better than what he was making, and there were hints of hefty annual increases. The whole environment seemed too good to be true. He could probably carve out a real niche for himself here, Alec thought; and he could surely advance within the organization. They had said as much.

He was elated when he received a firm offer. This was the career move he had been hoping for, and they seemed genuinely pleased to have him. In fact, a great deal of fanfare accompanied his arrival on the scene. A memo had been distributed to the entire staff, accompanied by his "bio" and a couple of samples of his work. His advance press was so good he wondered if he could live up to it.

The honeymoon turned out to be rather brief. It came to an end just as Alec was finishing up his first article on the company's president, which was to be submitted to a local magazine. He had always been a quick study, and the kind of consulting services this company offered its clients didn't seem all that complicated. He thought it was a pretty darn good piece, if he did say so himself.

The president apparently didn't agree. His critique, delivered in front of the senior writer, was the last thing Alec expected to hear. The president was polite but clearly disappointed that Alec had missed the point he wanted to make in this article. He thought he had been clear in his explanation. He was puzzled, he said, that the piece was so *off the mark.*

The senior writer—who had been quite personable and friendly during the interviews—just sat there, saying nothing, never changing his expression … except once, when a self-satisfied look seemed to flash across his face for one brief moment. Alec was sure he imagined it. The meeting was a disaster, leaving him a little shaken. But he was no stranger to criticism. It was part of being a writer. He went back to his office and rewrote the article.

It took *four* rewrites to get a final sign-off on the piece; and, by that time, Alec could barely recognize his own words, of which very few were left. As the president had become increasingly frustrated with Alec's inability to *get the point,* he virtually dictated the whole article, sentence by sentence. Now, Alec was more than just a *little shaken;* he was almost sick with self-doubt.

Had it been a one-time occurrence, or even two, he could have weathered the storm. But the scenario repeated itself over and over until Alec could barely write a sentence without knowing it would be picked to pieces, scrapped, and completely reworded.

He didn't know how to react or what to say. Nothing he said seemed to matter anyway. When he had tried to make a point, during a recent meeting, the president had suggested that *getting defensive was a poor way to respond to constructive criticism.* That was the problem. The criticism didn't seem very constructive to Alec; in fact, it seemed *de*structive. If that was its intent, it was working. He felt quite destroyed.

He tried to think it through logically. For seventeen years, he had been a respected writer. When this company hired him, its management acted as if they had snagged a prize. They made a big deal out of how talented he was and how pleased they were to have him on board. Now, only four months later, he felt like a complete failure, not to mention a fake. He wondered if he had ever been any good, if he really did have talent, or if he had somehow managed to fool everyone all those years and had finally been discovered.

The worst part was that he simply froze at the idea of writing. He was immobilized by his fear of failing again; of sitting through another humiliating meeting with the president rewriting his work; and the senior writer, who was always present, looking inscrutable and saying nothing. When he did speak, it was to point out that the meaning was unclear, or the point had been buried, or the paragraph didn't hang together, or some other equally deflating observation.

Alec resigned before he was fired. He was certain he would have been fired. He felt shell-shocked, and it took him quite a while to recover from the experience. Eventually, he did manage to see the short-lived job in some sort of perspective, to regain his confidence, and to realize that he was not an impostor or a failure. He began to write again, and, without the unrelenting criticism, recaptured his previous flare.

Alec never completely understood what went wrong at the consulting firm, though he had a few theories. All he knew for certain was that he could never have written anything that would have satisfied them, if he had died trying. He never could have pleased them, never have been able to read their minds, never have done what they *said* they hired him to do. Finally, he chalked it up to a colossal mismatch and tried to put the whole thing behind him.

What Went Wrong?

It appears that just about everything that could go wrong did in Alec's case, but perhaps the biggest hurdle he encountered was unclear and unexpressed expectations. The president clearly had something in mind, probably a duplication of the senior writer's style; but he never made that clear to Alec, during the interviewing process or in the meetings to critique Alec's work. If you don't know what is expected of you, you would have to be a magician to deliver it. A second major block was most likely *sabotage*. The senior writer didn't want any competition, so he eliminated it by subtly undermining everything Alec wrote. This obstacle was too big to get around and too deeply entrenched in the organization to overcome. In the end, it defeated all of Alec's efforts and created a lose-lose situation. The company lost, and Alec lost. There was, however, one winner: the senior writer.

Getting Past the Bridge Troll

George waited until Lou Ann stepped away from her desk before he rapped on the open door and asked, "Hey Phil ... got a minute?" It was a ridiculous way for a one vice-president to get some time with a peer, George knew; but it was far easier than trying to get on Phil's calendar or leaving a message or asking to be advised when he was free. None of those things ever happened, nor were they likely to happen as long and Lou Ann sat in front of that door, guarding Phil from any and all perceived attackers. She was, in fact, more effective at protecting her boss than the Secret Service was at protecting the President, George thought for probably the four hundredth time.

It's ridiculous that his calls are screened, that he only gets the messages Lou Ann feels are worthy of his attention, and that his time is portioned out to only the favored few, George was thinking as he walked into Phil's office. He was somewhat irritated, as he always was when he allowed himself to lurk around until that woman went to the ladies' room. Forget lunch. She *never* went to lunch. She ate at her desk so no one could slip by. But even Lou Ann had to go to the ladies' room occasionally; and, when she did, Phil always seemed to find himself deluged with unexpected visitors.

Carol sat at her desk, fuming. She was sure there must be steam coming out of her ears, and her face actually felt hot. She had to calm down, she told herself; but it was hard because Lou Ann made her so angry that she literally shook before, during, and after any encounter with her. Once again, Carol had somehow lost the battle. She felt not only dumb but abused.

What's wrong with this picture? she asked herself. I know Phil is a busy guy. He *is* the chief financial officer, this *is* the end of the fiscal year, and he *is* trying to get the final numbers out. But he's not God. When the president of the company wants to talk to him, he should be able to talk to him, right? Apparently this was not the case. *Phil is unavailable at this time ... Phil is away from the office ... Phil can't be reached right now,* were Lou Ann's usual responses.

Unavailable? Away from the office? How could he be away from the office when he has to do the final numbers? And why isn't a simple request from the president's executive secretary sufficient to get him on the line, or, at the very least, to get him to call back?

Of course, she would have to tell the president she hadn't been able to locate Phil, let alone get through to him. It would not be the first time, and she always felt so inept when this happened. Occasionally, he would tell her to forget about it and just pick up the phone and call Phil's office himself. And what do you know? He would actually get to talk to Phil. Maybe the president is on the "favorite person's list," Carol thought, but she doubted it. She wondered who was good enough to make that list. She wondered if there were such a list. She wondered how Lou Ann got away with it.

Emily was in a bind. The annual report was ready to go to the printer, except for the last-minute financials, which would have to be plugged into the book, proofed, approved, and sent to the printer within twenty-four hours. It was cutting it close, but they cut it close every year. That was the nature of the beast, and, with cooperation from finance, the communication department could make the deadline. Emily didn't miss deadlines, and this was one that *could not* be missed, under any circumstances. She knew that. Phil knew that. Even Lou Ann knew that.

She tapped her fingernails on the desk until the clicking brought her back to the present. She had called Phil three times already and come up against the bridge troll—Emily's name for Lou Ann—each time. *He was working on them and couldn't be disturbed. He was going over them with the corporate attorney. He had just finished them, and Lou Ann would personally get them to Emily as soon as she was able to break away.*

As soon as she was able to break away. What in the world does *that* mean? Emily wondered, as she pulled on her jacket and headed down the hall to Phil's office. What could be more important than this when you report to the CFO? Unless, of course, Lou Ann was on the phone with a financial analyst or *The Wall Street Journal*. That must be it: She's holding a press conference!

Emily caught herself in mid-thought and vowed that she was going to confront Phil with the facts, once and for all. She would let him know, if he didn't already know, what a one-woman obstacle course Lou Ann was. No one else seems willing to do it; so I will, she almost said out loud. But she could not possibly do it today. She had to get those financials to the printer. It would have to wait until she wasn't up against a deadline, until she had more time, until Lou Ann was on vacation, perhaps.

Going for MVP as Goalie

There is a Lou Ann in every company—a mountain of resistance to cooperation, productivity, and good business practices. There she or he sits, like a boulder in front of the entrance to the cave, preventing anyone from entering or anything from getting accomplished. The Lou Anns of the world are formidable, stopping everyone from secretaries to senior executive in their tracks. How do they get away with it? They have lots of help and support for their behavior. That's how.

Every single person in this story enabled Lou Ann to perpetuate her intolerable business behavior. For one thing, no one confronted her or Phil with the what was going on. For another, though they all fumed and fussed, they played her game by waiting until she was absent or allowing someone higher up in the pecking order to pull rank and get past her. There is no question that Lou Ann is a formidable hurdle, but with some strength and leverage, she could be dislodged. For some reason, no one is willing to lead the effort; and, as long as they continue to play the game, Lou Ann will continue to win.

Conclusion

This litany of obstacles, unfortunately, does not *begin* to scratch the surface of what can impede your progress, trip you up, and stand between you and what needs to be done. What is even worse is how much more the rule they are than the exception to the rule. Poor management, poor customer service, scrambled priorities, and enabling bosses—all the hurdles you encountered in these little vignettes—are not only common but accepted as "the way things are around here." If you have ever encountered such impediments to productivity, you know from first-hand experience that is *not* how things should be.

SECTION THREE

Dealing With Difficult People

CHAPTER ELEVEN

Understanding Behavioral Styles

Dr. Michael Cristiani, Managing Principal of Cristiani Consulting Group, helps companies match appropriate training to their strategic objectives, assists departments and functions in working more collaboratively, develops functioning teams, and trains internal consultants. He holds a masters and doctorate in counseling psychology. Before launching his own business, Dr. Cristiani held professional positions with an international training and consulting firm, a major aerospace company, and a manufacturer of medical devices. In each of these positions he has used behavioral models to help others understand how and why people act as they do and how to work together.

It's not news that people are different and operate differently. Various behavior models are an attempt to help people make sense of their own behavior and that of others. In the past, there was often an assumption that there was *one* best way of doing things, especially in the expert knows best aaproach. Over time, as we began to apply these theories to the workplace, we discovered that there was *not* one best way of being a leader or a manager. There are many different ways, just as there are many different circumstances or objectives.

The models we developed were simple so that people could use them to interact with each other more effectively. The disadvantage of these models is that human beings are not easily classified into one category or another. On the other hand, it isn't actually *people* we are classifying; it is their *behavior.* Some models are behavioral and focus on people's actions—what they *do*; others get more inside people's heads in terms of *why* they act the way they do.

Is there a right way to lead or interact? I think there are certain characteristics we can think of as fundamental in dealing effectively with others. For example, if you want to get along with people, you have to have an understanding and some empathy for their situation or their point of view. To me, that is a *principle*. Regardless of the model, I think it is an essential principle of dealing with people, no matter who they are or what their position in the organization.

Social styles were first introduced into the business arena by a company called Tracom Corporation out of Denver. One of Tracom's people, Larry Wilson, went out on his own and formed Wilson Learning, which also classified behavior based on identifiable styles such as "Driver." Another well-known model is the Managerial Grid, which measures task and people orientation. The Grid is numbered 1 to 9, with 1, 9 indicating high attention to people but low attention to tasks, and 9, 1 indicating a high inclination toward task management but low on people orientation. In other words, 9, 1s are focused on getting the job done; and 1, 9s are concerned with how the situation will affect people. A perfect balance between these two extremes would be 9, 9 in which a manager would give equal weight to people and tasks.

Some basic research that came out of Ohio University led to the Dimensional Model developed by Psychological Associates, in which different combinations of dominance, submissiveness, warmth, and hostility are used to classify various behaviors. In this model, the preferred behavior is a combination of dominance and warmth.

A very popular model, called the Myers-Briggs Type Indicator, catapulted into the mainstream after some work done in World War II. It is based on the theories of Carl Jung. It has been very well researched, but a caution is to avoid putting people in boxes. It is important to realize that people act in different ways, depending on the situation. The theory is that all of us have certain innate preferences and different degrees of them. When you have a preference for behaving in a certain way, you generally get better at it. It doesn't mean that you *can't* behave another way. It's like being right or left handed. Your preference might be to use your right hand, but you *can* learn to use the other hand if you have to.

Myers-Briggs has four main classifications of behavior types and 16 different possibilities for combining them. The descriptive terms in that model are now a little misleading. For example, in the first dimension, *introversion* and *extroversion* have different meanings than they ordinarily do. In this model they refer to how you focus your energy—internally or externally—and how you deal with the world. Do you focus on the outside world in terms of taking action, maintaining your networks, and being aware of your environment; or do you tend to conceptualize a problem internally, work it through in your head, and look deeply into issues?

The second dimension refers to how we gather information. One way is *sensing;* the other is *intuitive.* Sensing types look at facts and data. They understand the planning stages, the sequences, and the implementation. Intuitive types see the big picture, connections, and possibilities.

The third dimension gets at how we make decisions—what we do with the data we've gathered. It includes *thinking* and *feeling.* The thinking person is logical, uses cause and effect, considers the pros and cons of a particular plan of action, and spots inconsistencies. The feeling person, on the other hand, is tuned in to how people are going to react to what is going on and to understanding the human impact of the decision.

The last dimension can be described as lifestyle oriebtation. The two types are *judging* or *perceiving.* Judging types provide organization and decisiveness. They generate systems to make things happen. Those on the perceiving side of the model are open to new ideas, insights, and ways of doing things and tend to be more flexible if something goes wrong or breaks down. Js (as judging types are called) focus on details and want to move toward a conclusion. Ps (perceiving types) see possibilities and keep their options open. These are two very different approaches and explain why Js and Ps often get frustrated with each other.

The various sixteen combinations help people understand that everyone has different preferences and that there are pros and cons to each of those preferences. If you have a business problem or situation, you might choose a P to investigate it but prefer a J to help execute it.

We all operate with some assumptions about how and why people behave as they do. Looking at these models helps us open up to the possibilities and become less judgmental of others. We tend to judge people by our own standards, which we learn from our parents, our church or synagogue, our social and educational environment, our business environment, even our role as Americans. There are certain ways we do things that are culturally acceptable and others that are not. We are *trained.*

Part of what models do is show us that we are all trained differently and that some of us have some innate abilities and skills to do things in different ways. Rather than seeing differences as negatives, we begin to view diversity as a plus. We see, for instance, that for some problems, it is preferable to have a person who is open to possibilities; and for other problems, we might want someone who looks for closure and moves things to conclusion.

Depending on what the situation is, we should be able to link into the best skills, abilities, and preferences of the people around us. This broadens our scope and we learn from others. If someone is different from us, how do we adapt ourselves to that individual, while still keeping the integrity of who we are and what is important to us? How do we interact with someone so that his or her needs are met while, at the same time, our values are maintained? How do we use the "best" of everyone to acheive our common goals? Behavioral models help us answer those questions.

*   *   *

Why do people act the way they do? Why is your boss a marshmallow instead of a manager; or, at the other extreme, a good imitation of Attila the Hun, rather than a reasonable human being? Why does the person at the next desk always have a story to tell, pictures to show, or some irrelevant piece of news to pass along when you don't even care? Why, when you are gathering information on an important topic, does your team leader insist on making a decision about it *right this minute?* And why do you shake, scream, shut down, lash out, freeze up, or whatever you do when someone yells at you?

People act the way they do for many reasons, some as complicated as their genetic predisposition to certain traits and some as simple as the fact that they have a cold or were up all night with a sick baby. They may be having a bad day or a bad life; they may have been heavily influenced by Pollyanna as a child; they may be the sort of person who tries to make lemonade out of lemons; or they may travel around with a perpetual black cloud over their heads.

Often people's behavior is consistent and predictable. They just are the way they are, and you have come to expect certain reactions from them. Others are completely unpredictable—cheery one minute, snappy the next—keeping you in a state of high alert at all times. The question of *why* they react to certain situations and people one way or another has intrigued social scientists for years and has become a science all its own that is, to varying degrees of success, frequently applied in the business setting.

The attempt to describe, classify, and understand human behavior has led to the development of a number of behavioral models, some easy to understand and some requiring a Ph.D. in linguistics. This chapter will introduce a few of these models and try to help you make sense of your own behavior and the behavior of those with whom you interact every day.

Kirton-Adaption Innovation Inventory (KAI)

The foundation of Michael Kirton's Adaption-Innovation theory is that problem-solving style is a fixed, permanent part of one's personality. If we understand how someone thinks and approaches problems, we can better understand that person. KAI is based on the premise that cognitive style—the way one thinks—has a deep-seated influence on behavior. When people are forced to depart from their preferred cognitive styles, they tend to experience stress. In the workplace, people are constantly interacting with others who have very different cognitive styles. This can easily cause problems in communication and understanding, which, in turn, lead to problems in working together.

KAI has only two categories of people: adapters and innovators. In business, there seem to be an equal number of adaptors and innovators, though the preponderance of one type or the other may vary from the board room to the shop floor. Here are some of the differences between adaptors and innovators:

Adaptors

- tend to be precise, reliable, efficient, methodical, and disciplined
- are concerned with resolving problems rather than discovering them
- seek solutions to problems in tried and true ways
- reduce problems by improving the situation, increasing efficiency, and promoting continuity and stability
- are viewed as sound, safe, and dependable
- never get bored; highly accurate during long spells of detailed work
- rarely challenge rules and then only when assured of strong support
- tend toward self-doubt; react to criticism by conforming even more; vulnerable to social pressure and authority; compliant
- provide stability, order, and continuity when collaborating with innovators

Innovators

- are seen as undisciplined, tangential thinkers and unorthodox problem solvers
- first discover the problem, then discover how to solve it
- question all assumptions related to the problem and then turn it on its head
- upset settled groups; show irreverence for accepted views; are seen as abrasive and creators of discord
- have little regard for "the ways things are usually done here"
- are viewed as unsound, and impractical; often shocking to adaptors
- frequently challenge the rules; have little respect for past customs
- appear to have confidence, especially when generating ideas; don't require consensus to be sure, even when others disagree
- supply the task orientation; break with the past and accepted theory when collaborating with adaptors

Leadership Grid®

Robert R. Blake's and Jane Mouton's Leadership Grid® (which used to be called the Managerial Grid) provides a framework for understanding different types of leadership. Like other models, it has behavioral dimensions, in this case two: concern for production and concern for people. Blake and Mouton describe five different leadership styles in terms of how much emphasis is placed on each of those two dimensions on a continuum of 1 to 9. They feel that the most effective leadership is that which embodies a combination of high concern for production and high concern for people—what Dr. Cristiani described as a 9, 9. The five key leadership styles and their position on the Leadership Grid are as follows:

- *Team Management (9, 9)* Because of the leader's high concern for production *and* for people, relationships are based on trust and respect; employees are committed, interdependent, and share a stake in the organization's success.

- *Middle-of-the-Road Management (5, 5)* A leader's demonstrated average concern for both production and people produces average or adequate performance on the part of employees. The trick is to strike a balance between the need to get work out and the ability to keep employee morale at a satisfactory level.

- *Authority-Compliance (9, 1)* The leader's high concern for production and low concern for people keeps the focus on the efficiency of operations. This leader arranges work conditions so that the human element barely interferes with getting the work done.

- *Country Club Management (1, 9)* This leader has a low concern for production but a high concern for people. Of most importance to this person are the needs of employees and building satisfying relationships. The result is a friendly, comfortable work environment and work tempo with little sense of urgency about getting the job done.

- *Impoverished Management (1, 1)* When there is little concern for either production or people, minimum effort is expended to get required work done, employees feel alienated, and whatever energy is exerted is to keep from getting fired.

Myers-Briggs Type Indicator (MBTI)®

Isabel Briggs Myers and Katherine Cook Briggs began developing MBTI in the early 1940s. Their purpose was to make C. G. Jung's theory of human personality understandable and useful in everyday life. The essence of the theory is that much of people's behavior is more orderly and consistent than it may seem because it is based on the differences in the way people use their *perception* and *judgment.*

Perception is all the ways we become aware of things, people, events, or ideas. Judgment is how we reach conclusions about what we have perceived. MBTI helps identify people's basic preferences in these two areas so that we can understand our own behavior and appreciate the differences in personal styles.

As Dr. Cristiani explained, MBTI breaks preferences down into four dimensions that combine to describe 16 personality types. Each combination of four letters concisely captures the underlying patterns and behaviors of one personality type. Here is what the letters stand for:

- *Extraversion (E) or Introversion (I)* describe how and where we focus our attention. E focuses attention on and draws energy from the outer world of people and things, versus the inner world of ideas and impressions preferred by I.

- *Sensing (S) or Intuition (N)* refers to one's style of taking in information. *S* gathers data directly through the senses as facts, details, and precedents. *N* collects data indirectly through relationships, patterns, and possibilities.

- *Thinking (T) or Feeling (F)* is about making decisions. *T* decides based on objective, impersonal logic. *F's* decision making is more subjective, people-centered, and value-based.

- *Judging (J) or Perceiving (P)* refers to a choice between structure and flexibility. *J* has an outward preference for having things planned and organized, whereas *P* has a more flexible style based on staying open to options and possibilities.

More than three million MBTIs are administered every year in this country. It has also been translated into two dozen languages around the world. It is used for many purposes, including team building, problem solving, management and leadership development, planning education and curriculum, diversity and multicultural training, self-understanding, career exploration, relationship counseling, and organization development.

NEO Personality Inventory or Five-Factor Model

The NEO, or Neuroticism, Extraversion, Openness Personality Inventory, is a recent version of a model that has been evolving for many years. Originally called the Five-Factor Model, it has grown out of the efforts of many researchers over the years. This latest version owes much to the work of P.T. Costa, Jr. and R. R. McCrea. The major broad domains of the Five-Factor Model are:

- *Extraversion (E),* a preference for social interaction, and activity for activity's sake
- *Agreeableness (A),* orientation toward compassion and caring about others and away from antagonism
- *Conscientiousness (C),* a certain degree of organization and preference for goal-oriented activity
- *Neuroticism (S),* a tendency toward negative emotionality, instability, and inability to cope
- *Openness (M),* a tolerance for new ideas and new ways of doing things as well as an experiential orientation

Situational Leadership

One of the better understood models that explains leadership effectiveness as it relates to behavior was created by Paul Hershey and Kenneth Blanchard, both organizational theorists. Blanchard is also the author of several books, including the popular *One Minute Manager.* The situational leadership model looks at the relationship between a leader's behavior and a worker's readiness to perform certain tasks or to pursue particular objectives. The theory is that effective leadership and delegation of responsibility depend on a person's maturity. Hershey and Blanchard have developed a maturity scale to help managers delegate more effectively.

   • The *Directing Stage* (high task-low relationship) is one in which the boss has a job to be done and *tells* the employee to do it. At this first stage of maturity, people need to be told specifically what to do and to receive constant feedback on how well they are doing. Delegation doesn't work with these employees, who can become overtly or covertly hostile when they don't receive regular instructions and feedback.

   • In the *Coaching Stage* (high task-high relationship) the boss has a job to be done and *convinces* the employee to do it. This second stage is a step up on the maturity scale. Employees at this level must be sold on the idea or task before they will do the job, but then they don't need close supervision. They do, however, still need regular, positive and negative feedback because they don't know where this task fits in the larger scheme of things. People at this level benefit most from a leader who is able to recharge and motivate them by preparing them for what is coming next.

• *The Participating or Supporting Stage* (low task-high relationship) is one in which the boss and employee share in determining what needs to be done. People at this level have more confidence in their ability to define the task and what it will take to do it, but they can't be cut loose. They must be able to participate in the decision-making process with their managers, to try out their ideas and see if they will fly. Without input from the boss, these employees feel uncertain and insecure and may fall back to the Coaching Stage.

• Finally, in the *Delegating Stage* (low task-low relation-ship) the boss essentially tells the employee, "Here it is. Go to it," and then provides little direction or support. Employees at this level need only to be given a sense of what their man-agers expect of them, and they can take it from there. They don't need much feedback either, but they do need to touch base now and then to be sure they are on the right track.

There is one more element to the Hershey-Blanchard model and that is the *ability and willingness of employees* to go through the four stages of maturity just described. At the lowest end of the continuum, they are unwilling and unable to take responsibility for performing a certain task. At the second, they are willing but unable to do it. At level three, the employ-ees are able to do the job but unwilling to do it. And, finally, at level four, they are willing and able to do what is asked of them; and they feel confident about their ability to perform.

SYMLOG

A System for the Multiple Level Observation of Groups, otherwise known as SYMLOG, is one of the more complicated models because it examines any or all aspects of behavior and value systems of individuals, groups, whole companies, and even societies. Its strength is that it can focus on one particular level or area of interest or on many levels all at the same time.

If this model were applied to leadership training, for example, it would take a very different approach than many others do. Instead of putting all of the resources and energy into trying to make someone a more effective leader, SYMLOG would take a more holistic view. It would look at the group of people being led, the dynamics of that group, and the relationships among its members. All of these things obviously have an effect on the leader, but often they are overlooked. With this model, both get attention.

SYMLOG takes the process one step further by looking at this group in the context of all the other groups in the company and of the broader society of which the company is a part. As we have seen, a company's "culture" has a profound influence on behavior. So, there are many levels at work here. It all begins with the single leader and moves up the small group he or she leads; then it proceeds to all the groups that make up the organization, and, finally, to the larger community in which the company dwells.

Each of these levels has a life of its own, but it is also part of an interdependent system that touches and affects everyone involved. SYMLOG claims to be the only instrument in the world that applies this multiple-level, system-wide view to any situation.

There are many ways to use this model, including training and developing leaders; building teams; assessing organizational cultures; managing diverse work forces; re-engineering companies; planning; evaluating existing programs; conducting market research; improving customer relations; and helping companies through mergers, downsizings, and organizational change.

WIIFM, or What's In It For Me?

Believe it or not, the six behavioral models touched on in this chapter do not even begin to scratch the surface of what is available to companies that wish to do everything from helping their employees understand themselves better to solving organizational problems. A visit to your local library or the World Wide Web yields enough information to start your own consulting firm.

But the real question is, What do these models mean to you? How can they help you know yourself, change your behavior if you choose to, get along with someone who drives you crazy, or explain to your boss why you love (or hate) detail work or problem solving or working alone?

Of course, all of these models and dozens more are only useful if you really understand and can apply their classifications, dimensions, and comparisons to your situation. Often that takes a professional or a training program. But even in this brief journey through the behavioral sciences, you might draw some conclusions.

If you review the contrast between adaptors and innovators in the KAI model, you should have no trouble figuring which side best describes you, even if the description is not totally accurate. If you are in a leadership position, you will find Blake and Mouton's Leadership Grid enlightening; and, if you're not, it may help you to see your boss in a different light.

The best known of all of these models is the Myers Briggs Type Indicator. Many people have taken the test and can tell you at a drop of a hat what their letters are and what that means. (The author is an ENFJ, by the way.) There is a caveat here. If you want to know what your letters are, have the questionnaire administered and scored by a qualified professional. You might start with a visit to your company's human resources department.

The NEO or Five-Factor model, too, may help you better understand yourself and your coworkers, but a word of caution here. It is *behavior* you are labeling, not *people.* In the Hershey-Blanchard Situational Leadership model, you can probably identify both your boss's and your own styles. You can also figure out without much difficulty where you are on the maturity scale, where you want to be, and what you have to do to get there.

Finally, there is SYMLOG, which is definitely not a do-it-yourself-project. While it does focus on the individual in part, it is really more of an organizational tool than a way to evaluate your own behavioral style.

Conclusion

Behavioral models are interesting, educational, and fun. They can provide new understanding and insights into yourself and those for whom you work. If your company offers programs in any of those covered here, or those not mentioned, it could be worth your time to sign up for one.

Take two lessons away from this chapter. The first is that the more you understand about your own and others' needs, styles, and behavior, the better able you will be to communicate and form solid relationships.

The second is that no matter how many ways you slice up a model or classify behavior, *there are no right ways or wrong ways to be.* There is only how you are and how well that is working in your present situation. If it isn't working, the more you know, the better able you will be to change whatever you feel should be changed.

CHAPTER TWELVE

Managing the Unmanageable Boss

Pat Newby is administrative secretary to the vice-president of Gundaker Commercial Group's Brokerage Division. Her career has spanned more than 20 years in all phases of administrative work, most of it in the field of real estate. She is licensed in real estate sales and did sell for two years before returning to the office environment. She has worked for a wide array of bosses in her career; but one, in particular, still stands out in her mind.

I went to work for a gentleman with whom I had a good working relationship at another firm. He left that company and started his own business. I knew he was trouble from the start. Why I went to work for him I don't know. I liked him as a person, but I knew that he was probably going to be one of the most impossible bosses in the world. My experience there was short lived, approximately eight weeks. That is how impossible he was.

He had a real knack for entering a room and causing nothing but total chaos. He knew that he interfered with his own progress. He wanted desperately to change. He asked what he could do to change; he made promises; but he never put forth the effort. It was almost as if he got in his own way.

He lacked good leadership skills, and therefore everyone around him went in twenty different directions. It was a new company with no sense of direction, no cohesiveness. Anyone who came in and tried to organize things or set up systems failed because he always interfered with everything that person was doing.

He was a terrible manager. You could be in the middle of a meeting with him, and you knew he wasn't listening to you. He would start talking about something completely different— some personal thing that had nothing to do with the agenda for the meeting—which definitely confirmed that he hadn't been listening.

Oddly enough, his right-hand person was very much like him. I walked into her office once, and it was like a pig sty. You could not even get in the door. Her door was always closed, and now I know why. If I had seen that earlier, I probably would have run much sooner. I am exactly the opposite kind of person, and they drove me crazy.

The guy was excellent in his field, but he was *not* a good businessman. By that I mean that he didn't have a good understanding of what it took to make a business tick. He knew that was a critical component of the operation but would never give it the attention it required or let anyone else give it that attention. He was a complete distraction.

His job was to go out and get business and take care of existing business because he had a lot of connections in the real estate appraisal field. He was supposed to leave everything else up to my coworker and me. But he didn't. He always had his nose in everything because he needed to feel needed.

He did not give his employees enough space to do our jobs and do them well. I would set up a system, and he would ask about it and announce it to the staff. Then no one would follow it. No one was *expected* to follow it. When I left, he hired a temp until he could find someone to replace me. Actually, I think they just decided to shoot from the hip, go day to day, and rely on people within the company to pick up the slack when and if they could.

The only thing he did right was hold a weekly sales meeting. Of course, the directives from the meeting were never followed up or enforced. He yelled at me when others were not performing. He didn't have the courage to directly confront someone and say, "This is the direction you were supposed to be taking. You haven't accomplished this. Why not?" He would just vent all of his frustration at me.

I didn't know what to do, so I met with a coworker. I asked her for guidance. After we met, I realized that she wouldn't be much help to me. I tried to work on two projects. I attempted to organize them; I met with my boss; I reworked the systems so everyone else would be free to do what they had been hired to do. But he would never work with me. He could always tell people the value of doing things a certain way, but he couldn't get there.

It was the domino effect: "Well, he doesn't care, why should we?" His behavior affected all of us. When I went to work there he said, "I don't want this to be like the other place," which was militaristic. Then, he went too far in the other direction. It was too relaxed, and it didn't feel like a work environment at all.

When I left, I told him it was not a good atmosphere for me. He wanted to know *why*. I said I felt non-productive and had no sense of accomplishment, both of which were very important to me. I felt as though there was no improvement in sight. He agreed and admitted, "I don't know how to change." I think he hired me to help him to change. Could I have succeeded? My instinct tells me *no*.

I did learn to trust my gut feelings. I knew it wasn't going to work. Yet, I didn't listen to my gut. I told my husband I was going to take the job, even though I *knew* it wasn't going to work. I thought I could tame him. I couldn't.

When you find yourself working for a boss who can't be managed, my advice is recognize early on what you can accept. If you find it all unacceptable, move on. Some things just can't be changed and can't be managed. Accept it.

* * *

Unless you own your own company, if you have a job, you have a boss; and the impact that person has on your life is inestimable. There are all kinds of ways of looking at your relationship with your boss, some healthy and productive, others much less so. One way is to see this person as a tyrant, someone who has complete power over your security, well being, and work life. Another is to see him or her as an ineffective annoyance you must endure, sidestep, and tolerate. A third option is to assume this is a partner, someone with whom you work to bring benefit to both of you and to the company.

How you view your boss depends on many factors: his or her style, your style, the culture in which you work, your previous experiences with bosses, the nature of your work, your industry, and a host of others. If you have worked for any length of time, by now you surely know that most bosses don't have a clue about how to manage. They may be in a management position, but chances are they have developed their management style by the seat of their pants over the years; and, if they are ineffective, they don't know it. If your boss has been fortunate enough to go through management training, that is a plus but not necessarily a guarantee of competence.

In this chapter you will gain some insight into what makes bosses tick, why they manage the way they do, and what you can do to improve your relationship with yours. First, let's define terms. While it is not a good idea to stick labels on people, we all tend to put bosses in two categories, good and bad or, a little less pejorative, *effective* and *difficult.* Those in the effective-boss category enhance your ability to do your job, recognize your achievements, and focus on what is best for the department or work group. Those in the difficult-boss category, on the other hand, have the same effect as a virus. They promote discord, they undermine effort, and they diminish those who report to them.

An effective boss:

- has basic people skills and uses them
- communicates clearly and directly
- helps you set and attain goals
- takes the time to listen to you
- delegates work and then gets out of your way and lets you do it
- respects herself and you

- is a risk taker
- builds *esprit de corps* and encourages teamwork
- brings a sense of purpose to the department or work group

A *difficult boss:*

- hogs the credit and the spotlight
- intimidates employees
- makes people so miserable that they quit
- sabotages or squelches your career
- talks about people behind their backs
- plays one-upmanship
- is threatened by a smart or talented subordinate

Name That Boss

Bosses come in "all shapes and sizes," meaning that, even within the black-and-white, good boss/bad boss categories, there are many shades of gray. What follows are descriptions of bosses we have known and loved, or been unable to love, and some ideas for how to manage them.

The Tyrant

There is no question that dictators get things done; but, whether they know it or not, their management style is as obsolete as the horse and buggy. With all of the recent down-sizing and layoffs, many of these old-school despots have been swept out the door. If your boss is one who has survived the purge, however, this news may be small comfort to you.

Some tyrants are the way they are because this is the only management style they have ever been exposed to, as well as the one top management condones because it gets results. Others are simply angry people who have never learned to control their emotions or to channel their anger in a more constructive way. Whatever the reason, this kind of boss can make your days a nightmare with his volatility, verbal abuse, and intimidation. He can also portray you to others as incompetent, lazy, dishonest, or disruptive, which won't enhance your chances of being recruited by another manager.

If your reaction to a tyrannical boss is to fight back or to disappear into the woodwork, frankly, neither approach is very productive. What you must do instead is try to prove your value to someone else in the organization, some other manager who may appreciate your abilities and go to bat for you. What else can you do to survive?

- You can find a release for your own frustration by talking it out with someone you can trust. That could be a friend, a coworker you are very sure of, another manager, or a counselor in the Employee Assistance Program (EAP), if your company has one. If this is a harassment issue, you should seek legal advice.

- You can do your job to the best of your ability no matter what the internal atmospheric conditions; keep copies of everything you do; and document, document, document. No one likes to live this way; but, if you think you may be in jeopardy, you have no choice.

- You can skillfully confront your boss when his behavior is offensive or abusive. You can ask for evidence to back up any accusations he may make. You can refute his statements with documentation. Or, you can simply leave the room.

- You can bring a neutral party with you to hear and observe what is said, go over your boss's head, or file a grievance. If you do any of these, though, be aware that you are declaring war. If you do go over his head, be well armed with evidence to support your claims.

- You can request a transfer to another department; or, of course, you can leave the company.

The Incompetent

If your boss can't manage her way out of paper bag, you are probably frustrated much of the time. Besides wondering how in the world she got this far in the company, you may be quite sure you could do her job better than she's doing it with one arm tied behind your back. As she bumbles through the day, avoiding decisions, barely communicating, and doing her best not to make waves, your department drifts along like a rudderless boat.

Needless to say, she has no idea how she is perceived and probably believes herself to be quite competent. She may launch fact-finding efforts, form committees, and create teams; but these are all delay tactics to keep her from having to *do* something. You may get the feeling that she is trying not to be noticed, to just blend in with the furniture and, in a way, she is. Often she doesn't meet your eye but looks off in some other direction when she speaks. When you talk she may interrupt you or clearly demonstrate by her response that she hasn't heard a word you said.

This person doesn't like arguments or conflict. She may be afraid she will have to mediate or that she will be bested by a subordinate. As a matter of fact, she *always* feels at risk. She is afraid a more capable person on her staff might displace her, afraid that if she makes a decision it will be the wrong one, afraid she will be blamed for any mistake one of her people makes. It's tough to live one's life in fear, but essentially that is exactly what she does.

If you are convinced your boss is in over her head, check with others in your department to see what they think. When you do this, seek out facts and evidence, not put-downs or gossip. Unless you find out that her days are numbered, you must deal with the fact that she is here, and you have to work for her.

- Try to determine how others see her without contributing to the rumor mill.
- See if you can get a feel for whether her job is in jeopardy or she is here to stay.
- Don't let her embarrass herself. Try to keep her shielded from situations in which she might show her weaknesses.
- Do what you can to direct her efforts and help her get organized by taking on more responsibility.
- Document your work as evidence of your capabilities.
- Apply for another job within the company.
- Talk to someone you trust in the human resources department.
- If you are stuck, and this looks like a long-term reality, consider going elsewhere.

The Patriarch (or Matriarch)

If you want to be nurtured, there is no better boss for you than the one who thinks managing is just another word for parenting. Whether or not he grew up watching *Father Knows Best,* he certainly believes it. He feels a great sense of responsibility for his little group of employees, just as he does for his children; and he runs the same tight ship at the office as the one at home.

Paternal bosses can have two sides: On one hand they are tough task masters—exacting, demanding, often disapproving. They want you to live up to your potential and make them proud of you. Your behavior reflects on their ability to manage. On the other hand, they turn into Florence Nightingales when you are sick, insisting that you go home, recommending doctors, and doing everything but bringing you chicken soup.

So, what's wrong with that? Well, for one thing, it is inappropriate. You are not his child; you are his subordinate. There is a difference. For another, he may not be the kind of parent you had or want. Or perhaps he is very much like your parent and that doesn't bring up warm, fuzzy thoughts for you. If you have less-than-beautiful memories of your childhood, having a patriarchal boss could bring up all sorts of responses.

If he views you as one of his kids, he is not treating you as an equal or as a competent adult. If you are a woman, he may not take you seriously, he may be a bit too patronizing. If he does view you as a pseudo-daughter, he may not see anything wrong with ordering you around and having you fetch coffee and do errands for him. If you are a man, he will want to test your stripes and shape you up—not always in a gentle manner. In either case, his attitude toward you may undermine the respect others in the organization have for you. When the going gets tough, he may abandon his paternal persona and turn mean.

There is a bright side to having this kind of boss. He could be a great parent who encourages his people and manages a work group that functions like one big happy family. When you do a good job, you get praised; if you goof up, you get a "little talking to." When you've proved yourself, you get promoted. This is a nice scenario. *Déja vu,* or welcome to the family you never had, working for a patriarch requires a strategy. Here are some things you should keep in mind:

- You are an adult and a professional. In this situation, remain aware of that and never slip into childish behavior.

- Keep you emotions under control. Don't cry or fight back. Keep your cool even in the middle of a confrontation. Some people can't stand tears, and others overreact to anger.

- If this person is a mentor, it will be a particularly tough to hold your ground. Be appropriately respectful but not obsequious. Maintain your sense of self.

- Don't let the conversation get too personal; don't spill your deepest, darkest secrets to him or listen to his. Try to keep all conversations on a profession level.

- Strive for independence and avoid ever appearing to be dependent.

The Cheerleader

There are some people who simply *attract* us, draw us in, and turn us on. They have a special presence about them, a kind of magnetism. Their energy is quite literally contagious and their effect inspiring. If they use this gift for the benefit of their people and the company, they are worth their weight in gold. If you work for such a person, you know she can iron out any disagreement, forge you and peers into a cohesive team, see your potential even when you don't see it, and help your career in many ways.

She can be a wonderful mentor, inspiring you to reach for the stars, steering you around land mines, and jump-starting your career. She can praise you for a job well done, help you overcome weaknesses, and shine the spotlight on you so that others can observe your contributions. Somehow, these people communicate their visions to us and bring us along for the ride as they strive to fulfill them. If your boss has a vision, notice how seductive it is, how you have embraced it, and the sense of purpose it gives you.

Is she too good to be true? Is this boss real, or did *you* imbue her with all of these wonderful characteristics? Unless she is an academy-award caliber actress, she is probably real, but there is a possible downside to an engaging and thoroughly likable boss. She knows she has charisma, and she uses it. She can charm her way out of anything. Though she is a born leader, she isn't always a team player. She can see the big picture but becomes bored by the details. What is the role you should play with this boss?

- You can be proactive, self-empowered, and self-motivated. If she doesn't bother with details, *you* become an expert at them.

- Always make her look good. Support her consistently, and reinforce her positive image in the organization. Be a fan. Be *her* cheerleader.

- Be honest and up front. Give her feedback on how you feel, how others feel, on what's going on in your department or work area.

- Share your knowledge, talent, information, and expertise with her. Anything you have that will help her will eventually bounce right back and help you. It's funny how that works.

The Addict

If you find your boss's behavior inexplicable, particularly after lunch; if he is frequently late in the morning or prone to miss Mondays; if he seems to have lost his "edge," you *may* be reporting him to a drug or alcohol abuser. Of course, unless he is falling down drunk or completely spaced out, both of which are unlikely, there is no way to know for certain. There are, however, some unmistakable signs.

Have you ever walked past his office and seen him napping? Does he share his personal or financial difficulties with you a little too freely? Are his mood swings erratic and frequent? Does he verbally abuse those who work for him? Does he seem unusually depressed? Have you ever smelled alcohol on his breath? Does he drink excessively at company events?

Even if you are quite certain that your boss is an alcoholic or a drug abuser, you are in a pretty difficult position. On one hand, "blowing the whistle" could jeopardize your job, especially if you are wrong. Conversely, turning away and pretending nothing's wrong or knowing something is wrong but choosing to remain silent is costly.

The company pays in terms of lost productivity and poor management; you pay because your leader clearly is not leading; the customer or client pays because anything anyone in an organization does ultimately affects the customer in some way. Most of all, your boss pays—with his health, his reputation, his career, his family, and perhaps his life. What can you do?

- Realize the volatility of this situation and your position in it.

- Be careful; don't put him or yourself at risk.

- Don't diagnose the problem. Just because you suspect alcoholism doesn't mean you are right or that you are equipped to deal with it.

- If your company has an EAP, request an appointment; lay out your concerns, supported by documented facts and ask for help.

- Maintain an attitude of concern and compassion for your boss.

- Insist on confidentiality, which is a given with an EAP. Often, once the situation has been reported, the EAP will take it from there and you will be out of the loop.

- If your company doesn't have an EAP, you have two choices. One is to seek help from someone you trust in the human resources department.

- The other is to request a private meeting with your boss, tell him what you have observed, and express your concern for his well-being. (This is difficult and risky.)

- Keep the conversation focused on facts and behaviors, not on him. You might say, "I've noticed that when you arrive in the morning, your eyes are red, and you don't look well." or "You seem to lose your temper frequently and, when you do, you say some very hurtful things.

That's not like you." Do *not* say, "I think you have a drinking problem; let's talk about it."

Switching Places and Perspectives

Empathy means truly understanding how another person feels. Can you say that you do understand how your boss feels? Do you know what she needs from you? Try to imagine that you are in her shoes, and her suit, and her office. How do you feel? What do *you* need?

If you are having trouble answering that, it may help to know your boss would, too. If you asked her what she needs, she might not be able to give you a list. However, if you look at it logically, she needs what every boss needs: people she can trust, who do their jobs well, who are good communicators, who run interference when necessary, and who understand the demands of her job.

These fundamental requirements cannot be a surprise to anyone, yet few people think about them, much less attempt to meet them. What does it take to have your boss trust you? Probably exactly what it takes to have you trust her. It means that when she tells you something, it stops with you. If she makes a mistake and you know about it, you make sure no one else knows it; and, if you can, you do everything you can do to *prevent* a mistake from happening in the first place.

It means that when you say you will do something or be somewhere, she can consider it done. It means you show up for work—body, mind, and spirit—every day; you know your job; and you do your job. It means your boss knows you're there for her, in attitude as well as in physical presence; that you will do nothing to undermine her; and that you will do everything to protect her professional image and reputation.

To do your job well, at the very least, means you have the education, training, and skills it takes to perform the required functions. The *way* you perform them has a tremendous bearing on the way *she* performs, because your work provides the foundation upon which her work is built. In addition, your performance reflects directly on her ability as a manager.

To do your job well, at the very most, means going beyond the basics and constantly stretching yourself and the limits of your job description by learning more, taking on more responsibility, and being proactive and self-empowered.

To be a good communicator takes desire, skill, education, and sensitivity. We are born with the capacity to communicate in any language and, perhaps, a predisposition to do it extremely well. But the rest depends on what we are taught by others and how we use those lessons in our lives.

The basics of communication are listening, speaking, writing, and sending and receiving nonverbal cues. In today's business environment, they also include computer savvy and knowing your way around a wide range of software programs; expertise in other industry-related technology; and knowing how to plan, organize, and conduct effective meetings.

To run interference when necessary means you are the screen through which others must pass before they have access to your boss. You protect her time, her privacy, and her space. Depending on her preference, that may include screening her calls, keeping her appointment book, and being the clearinghouse for all messages. There are pluses and minuses to this responsibility. On the plus side, your judgment is trusted and respected; you have a great deal of responsibility; you are a valued member of her team.

On the minus side, you could be overwhelmed with just this set of duties; if you're not careful, you can develop an unrealistic sense of your own importance; or you may incur the dislike of those who want to get through and find you an obstacle to their goals.

To have a pretty good idea of what it takes to do her job means not only her actual day-to-day responsibilities, her relationship with her own boss, and the level of expertise she must possess, but also the *stress-producing* aspects of her position. The first three may engender respect, if she is handling them well, or disdain, if you feel she is not. The last one should help you develop empathy. If there is stress in your job, you can assume there is stress in her job. Stress seems to be a universal byproduct of working. Hers may be different from yours, greater or lesser, more or less important in your eyes. But stress is in the eye of the beholder, and it takes its toll. If you understand her stressors, you will be more tolerant and in a better position to help minimize them.

Speaking of Stress

To live is to experience stress. If you don't, you are quite literally dead. To work is to heap a little more stress on top of what you already have. To work for a difficult boss could put you in the danger zone. This must be a pretty obvious observation, since bookstores have whole sections devoted to just this topic. Since stress is a fact of life and is hazardous to your health in every conceivable way, it just makes good sense to arm yourself with some techniques for diffusing it before you implode.

Everyone knows, or should know, that eating a balanced diet, getting adequate rest, exercising regularly, and programming fun into your life are the basics of stress reduction, not to mention overall good health. But even if you make every effort to live a healthy lifestyle, you need some more specific, effective, and instant ways to get through really tough situations. What can you do right this minute?

Brandon Toropov, author of *The Complete Idiot's Guide to Getting Along With Difficult People* and *The Art & Skill of Dealing With People,* suggests these ten instant stress busters: Watch your breathing; drink water; know your A, B, Cs; make a mental list; turn on the radio—in your head; freeze; use your survival skills; restate the orders; volunteer to make commitments and then keep them; and, finally, use humor. All of these ideas can work wonders, says Toropov, *if* you take a moment or two out of your day to practice them. That's the catch and the key. Taking the time is actually more difficult for many people than any of the techniques.

Deep diaphragmatic breathing is an instant calmer-downer. Sit, stand, or lie down; and simply inhale, starting in your stomach and ending in your chest. Then exhale slowly, first emptying the chest and then stomach. A few slow, deep breaths like these will have a dramatic effect on your stress level. Water is recommended in every single health promoting program and weight reduction diet. The key here is not only to drink it but to *focus* on drinking it. Don't just mindlessly gulp it down; concentrate.

One of the most powerful methods of stress reduction being practiced today is meditation, a word that is beginning to sound far less foreign and mystical to Westerners than it once did. There are countless types of meditation, but all of them seem to have the effect of calming the mind and easing the body. Dr. Jon Kabat-Zinn, director of the Stress Reduction Clinic at the University of Massachusetts Medical Center, uses meditation with patients who come to the clinic with every sort of problem from depression to chronic pain to cancer.

Conclusion

In his book, *Full Catastrophe Living: Using the Wisdom of Your Body and Mind to Face Stress, Pain, and Illness,* Dr. Kabat-Zinn explains, "The *full catastrophe* captures something positive about the human spirit's ability to come to grips with what is most difficult in life and to find within it room to grow in strength and wisdom. ... To some extent our ability to influence our circumstances depends on how we see things."

Part of the power of meditation is that it changes the way we see things, our interpretation of events and their importance to us. The problem may not be so much that your boss is difficult; it may be more the way you see and deal with that difficulty.

CHAPTER THIRTEEN

Getting Uncooperative Coworkers to Cooperate

Lois LaDriere is the longest tenured, senior-level, law firm marketer in St. Louis and one of the first two in Missouri. As a pioneer in this rapidly growing profession, she is the director of marketing for a prestigious international law firm. Working for 187 independent bosses, Ms. LaDriere has become adept at the art of persuasion and negotiation.

A law firm, by nature, has a dysfunctional structure in which all of its shareholders or partners share in the decision-making process. It is often difficult to get lawyers to cooperate with someone in my position for several reasons: in one sense they are my peers, and in another sense they are my bosses. Moreover, I am trying to get them to do things they don't have time for or much incentive to do. The only resources I have are my credibility and the respect I have attempted to build over the years. It is only through their respect for my judgment, sense of fairness, knowledge, and experience that they will listen to me.

While they do listen to me now, I must admit they didn't for the first few years. Although I have now been at the firm for six years, I realize this is a long-term project that requires a lot of patience. But it can be very frustrating because I continually need to be persuasive; remain positive; utilize my sense of humor; and, at the same time, gain their respect.

I would like to think I was hired because my firm was proactive—more proactive and progressive than any other firm in Missouri. Fortunately, the leaders of the firm have good business sense and are more sophisticated than our competitors. They realize that in order to stay ahead of the curve they needed to differentiate, to distinguish themselves from their competitors. Part of that effort includes raising awareness among the business community and separating ourselves from the competition.

In most firms about a third of the attorneys are proactive marketers, a third are borderline, and a third are opponents of marketing altogether. The most important part of my job as marketing director is not necessarily doing traditional marketing, but rather educating those who are borderline in an effort to move them into the proactive camp. The true nay-sayers I leave alone, preferring instead to focus on the positive attorneys who are interested and really need my help.

Most often, I initiate the marketing relationship with our attorneys, whom I consider to be my clients. If I am doing my job effectively, I am proactively asking, "What do you need?" and "How can I help you?"—if time and resources permit. Sometimes I have neither time nor resources. Then the firm, as a whole, must address some issues. If it determines we need to focus on bringing in more business, the time and resources situation usually improves.

Although all partners share in the decision-making process, our chairman and managing partner are the two most powerful and influential people in the firm. We also have an executive committee comprised of ten well respected partners who make decisions for the firm. With 187 shareholders, however, it is life by committee, which involves a long and tedious process to reach any decision.

To expedite the decision-making process, I frequently approach the influencers first to engage their support. Remember, they must manage by persuasion, too. That is really what law firm management is about.

Essentially, I am trying to convince all of our attorneys to allow me to do what I was hired for. I accomplish that on several levels. When a client—one of our attorneys—has a need, I work with that person individually. That's one way.

Another way occurs when a practice group has a need. We have 20 practice groups. I attend almost all of their monthly meetings, during which they discuss current projects, new legislation, topics of interest to clients, and information we should be providing our clients because we have a *duty to inform.* Marketing grows out of that duty to inform our clients. That's why some of my counterparts in other law firms have such titles as client services director or client coordinator.

We discuss ideas generated during those meetings, and we ask a lot of questions. "Is this idea newsworthy and timely?" "Does it warrant distributing a bulletin or a client alert?" "What is the best way to get the word out?" "Are we targeting existing clients or prospective clients?" We identify our audience and strategy first, recommend the best approach, and then implement it.

Attorneys have little understanding of the process and effort involved in holding a function or staging a special event. For example, recently we were discussing a COBRA issue that affects our clients' pensions plans. One attorney suggested we should inform our clients through a seminar to be held in early May. We were having this discussion in *April.* He didn't think about giving invitees three weeks' notice. He didn't think about finding and booking a facility. He didn't think about allowing adequate time to design and print invitations and materials.

In situations like this one, it's important to ask, "How much notice do you think we should give invitees?" Then I work backwards to see how much time we really need. In this case, I never said, "This won't work because we don't have enough time." But, as we worked back through the calendar, the attorney realized our predicament and suggested that we schedule the program at a later date.

That same day, another attorney spoke at a meeting about getting the word out concerning a matter of interest to clients, but felt that it *wasn't really a marketing issue.* Of course, we all knew that it *was* a marketing issue. I guess I still have some educating to do.

*   *   *

In your relationship with a peer, you are not the boss; she is not the boss. Neither one of you has any real "power" over the other. In theory, you enjoy equal status. In theory, too, you should *want* to help each other when a need or an opportunity arises. In practice, however, you may be finding that getting this person to help or even to go along with the program is next to impossible. Whether your coworker marches to her own drummer, has a wide streak of independence, prefers competition to collaboration, or is just plain antisocial, she is certainly not what one would describe as a team player.

Few of us do our jobs as if we lived on an isolated island. People in companies, departments, and work groups have to cooperate with each other, or the whole complex system of "getting things done" will eventually break down. Relationships, of course, are neither simple nor predictable. There are few hard-and-fast rules for getting along or for getting things done *with* other people. Even if you had the power—if this person were your subordinate rather than your peer—wielding that power would not be the best way to engage her cooperative spirit. True, you would get things done; but chances are it wouldn't be *with* her.

Just because you are supposedly on equal footing in your organization does not mean you have no tools to assist you. There are many things you can do to get an uncooperative coworker to cooperate. In this chapter you will find a veritable smorgasbord of strategies to choose among.

Identifying the Players

How you deal with a recalcitrant coworker depends on a number of factors, including your personal style, her personal style, the immediate circumstances, the corporate culture, and other people's effect on the situation. Let's start with your style. As you've already seen in the chapter on behavioral systems, there are many models out there to help you identity your own preferred behavioral style.

Technically, no one has any power in a peer-peer relationship. There is quite literally a power vacuum. For a strong person, who is used to exercising control, this can be very frustrating. Let's say that description fits you. The first thing you might try is filling that vacuum by assuming power. You could do that by being openly competitive or dominant; you could simply ignore the other person; or you could assume a patronizing attitude in an attempt to gain the advantage by undermining her confidence.

On the other hand, let's assume you are not comfortable being in control and avoid such situations whenever you can. The last thing in the world you're going to do is vie for something you don't want. All you do want in this situation with your coworker is to avoid pain, to come out of it no worse than you were when you began. You may not have a very high opinion of your fellow worker. Perhaps you think she is not too bright or doesn't follow the rules or is trouble looking for a place to happen. You may be more suspicious than that, seeing this particular individual as shrewd, self-serving, and dangerous. *If she wants power, fine,* you may think. *Let her have it.*

A third possibility is similar to the second one in that you don't want power, not because it's uncomfortable but because you would prefer that no one had it. Power, in your mind, gets in the way of everyone getting along like a smoothly functioning team. Your aim in life, and especially in this situation, is to promote a harmonious relationship with your peer so that together you can get the job done and, above all, remain friends.

Finally, you may be the kind of person who doesn't seek power but who won't run from it if it comes your way. Like the previous example you, too, opt for teamwork and good working relationships; but you don't close your eyes to reality. If your peer doesn't share your goals, you are willing to face that fact and apply one of the many strategies offered in this chapter.

As you can see, your *attitude* toward your peers is a key factor in the approach you will take to convince one of them to work with you. Another equally important consideration is your peer's style. Whatever your style may be, it will have to be adapted to the person you're trying to influence.

Let's say your colleague is the one who must be in control of circumstances. Whether power is an issue to you or it isn't, you know it is an issue to her—a big issue. While you're trying to get a dialogue going, she is turning your interaction into a contest she is determined to win. If you're not careful about how you handle this, the whole discussion could turn into a game of one-upmanship or, worse, an argument you both may regret.

If the person you are trying to influence would rather avoid the whole idea of collaboration and be left alone, you may find that more difficult to handle than the competitive type. This person could be skittish about taking a risk of any kind. Somehow, you're going to have to make her feel safe. One way to do that is to slow your speech and just take your time. Don't get impatient; don't push; just gently persuade. And try to keep her involved in the conversation. If you don't, you may find that you are doing all the talking, and she is either resistant or putting up a wall or just caving in to avoid unpleasantness.

If your coworker is no problem and seems eager to work with you on anything, that may look like the best of all possible worlds—until you look more closely. Ask yourself if her style is to *always* cooperate, *always* go along, *always* say, "Sure I'll do it." If the answer is *yes,* you won't be sure if she is really on board or just trying to keep you happy. While what you want is a willingness to cooperate, if it comes too easily, it pays to dig a little deeper. Acquiescence is not the objective; collaborative engagement is.

Your coworker may be a sharp, savvy business person who will go along with the program *if* you can convince her it is in your mutual best interest to do so. You may have to work a lot harder to get her cooperation; but, if she signs on, it's for real and for the long haul, which is what you really want.

Painful Peer Relations

Even if you are not trying to create a collaborative work environment at the moment, your problem may be one of just trying to coexist on the same planet with a very difficult person—someone with whom you can find no common ground and who seems bent on making your life at work a living hell. Take heart. There *are* ways to work with this person; and, though you may never be best friends, at least you can avoid being worst enemies. Here are a few suggestions that might help the situation:

1. *Don't psychoanalyze this person.* You are not a therapist; and, chances are, you would be way off the mark if you tried to be one. If you are able to give your peer the benefit of the doubt you might assume that, either something is going on in her life and her behavior has *nothing* to do with you, or that your relationship has gotten off track somewhere along the way and her behavior has *everything* to do with you.

2. *Risk confronting the issue.* The only way to know what is wrong is to ask, which is probably the last thing you want to do. But if you are able to say something like, *I sense some tension between us, which really disturbs me. I'd like to know if I've done something to offend you. If I have, I will do whatever I can to remedy that situation.* This is not an attack on her or her behavior; it is more of a process check and, thus, pretty unthreatening. Best-case scenario, she may tell you that you have done nothing and that she has things on her mind or that you have done something and here is what it is. Worst-case scenario, she tells you nothing, and you are right back where you started, except that you know you tried.

3. *Don't get personal.* The best way to exacerbate a problem is to personalize it in one of two ways. Either *you* take the conversation personally and get your feelings hurt or you attack the other person and hurt her feelings. Statements

like, *You have an attitude problem,* or *You are an informa-tion bottleneck that is slowing down the entire department,* or *We lost the account because you missed the deadline* are blaming, attacking statements. Using the word *you* should act as a red flag that alerts you to stop, rethink, and if possible reword your statement.

4. *Stick to the issues, and soften your rhetoric.* Think about presidential debates or a heated discussion on the Senate floor or contract negotiations between labor and man-agement. In each case it is *policies* or *points of view* or *issues* that are attacked, as opposed to people. In all of these exam-ples, strong emotions are definitely voiced, but they are also carefully packaged. It isn't phony or dishonest to package your remarks; it is diplomatic and good business. We can accept some pretty tough talk *if* it's delivered the right way and we don't feel personally assaulted.

5. *Practice assertive communication.* When we are angry or frustrated it is easy to forget everything we ever knew about how to express ourselves in the right way. Our tendency is to become aggressive and dominate the other per-son or to become passive and capitulate without a fight. In the middle, of course, is keeping our heads and being assertive, neither of which come naturally in the heat of an emotional conversation. Assertiveness is built on a foundation of respect: respect for yourself and respect for the other person. If you cultivate those two attitudes you will never become aggressive or passive. If you respect yourself, you won't become defen-sive and cave in under attack. In fact, you won't allow yourself to *be* attacked. If you respect the other person, you won't go on the offensive. Rather, you will find some way to state your position without belittling the other person in the process.

6. *Build a support system.* There are times when you will need others to help you through a particularly tough sit-uation. Calling on team members for short-term support is quite different from putting together a permanent group of allies to back you up in your ongoing battle with another per-

son. First of all, you shouldn't be engaged in an ongoing battle. Office feuds are costly in terms of energy, morale, and productivity. It takes two to feud. You have no control over your peer, but you do have control of yourself. You can simply refuse to play the game.

Ten Ways to Improve Communication

Much of what goes wrong between people in a work setting, or in any setting, is the result of poor communication. You send a message, thinking it is very clear. After all, *you* know what you meant. But the recipient of your message, for some reason, doesn't get what you sent. In your mind, she has "misinterpreted" your words; and you can't imagine how that could have happened. In her mind, there was no other possible way to interpret it. The fault is yours for not saying what you meant. If you are not able to clear up the misunderstanding, you have fertile ground in which to grow a problem. What follows are some suggestions for improving your communication skills:

1. *Ask before you tell, listen before you speak.* There may be no more valuable rule than this one, and yet few of us heed it. If we were honest, we would admit that nothing is quite as appealing as the sound of our own voices or as compelling as our opinions. Of course, it never occurs to us that the person we are talking to feels exactly the same way about *her* voice and opinions. If we focused on that truth for a moment we would see how simple communication could be. All we really have to do is *let the other person talk first.* Yet, we rarely do that. Instead, we begin our conversations by telling how *we* feel, what *we* think, what *our* objectives are, often having no idea how our peer feels, what *she* thinks, or what *her* objectives are. If you take no other suggestion away with you from this chapter, take this one. It can revolutionize your interpersonal relationships.

2. *Remember these two important questions: What do* you *think?* and *What are you trying to accomplish?* There is power in these questions, not only in asking them but in listening, truly listening, to the answers. There is power in wanting to know and in tailoring your response to what you hear rather than what you think. There is power in taking control of the situation by posing the questions in the first place. There is power in focusing on the other person and not on yourself. There is power in letting your peer know that what she has to say is important to you.

3. *Be absolutely sure you received the message the other person sent.* What you hear and how you interpret what you hear are not always what the speaker intended, which is how communication goes awry.   How often have your responded to someone's remark only to have her say, *That's not what I meant?* It is so easy to find out what she did mean, if you actually got it, or if you missed it by a mile. All you have to do is *repeat the message back in your own words* and ask, *Is that right?* If it is, the other person will say, *Absolutely;* if it isn't, she will correct you immediately. That applies to the content part of the message. Equally important is the emotional or feeling side of the message. If the words you hear are civilized and calm but the body language is tense and angry, which should you believe? The nonverbal communication is probably the more accurate of the two, but here again you can check out your interpretation. It has become a cliché by now; but no line better illustrates this idea than, *You seem upset.* If the person is upset, you will soon know it by her response. You will probably also know why.

4. *Check for receptivity.* You are ready to confront a troublesome issue or have a serious talk with your coworker, so you walk over to her desk and launch your monologue. Right? Wrong ... for two reasons. First, it breaks rule number one: *Ask before you tell, listen before you speak.* Second, it could be the worst of all possible times to have this conversation. She may be in the middle of a project, overwhelmed with

work, preoccupied with another issue, not feeling well, or reeling from a lecture from her boss. In other words, she is not ready to have the little talk you want to have right now. If you insist on having it, you will have, at the very least, wasted your breath and, at the very most, sabotaged your own best intentions. How do you know if this is a good time? Ask.

5. *Don't be a conduit for every piece of juicy gossip you hear.* There aren't too many reasons to pass along information you hear or observe or were told in confidence. One is that the information refers to some unethical or illegal activity; but, beyond that, not much news is worth being labeled as gossip. If you think passing along a great little story makes you look like you're in the know, think again. As revered as the grapevine may be in your office, it really isn't the most effective way to convey information up, down, or sideways. In fact, gossip is a little like the children's game of telephone. The first child in line whispers a secret to the next child, who whispers it to the next one and so on down the line. Everyone laughs when they hear how the secret has changed since it was first whispered, but that is just the point. You hear something and pass it along, that person passes it along; and, by the time the fifteenth person gets it, it bears no resemblance to the original statement. At best, it might seem humorous, but, at worst, it could result in a great deal of harm. Let gossip stop with you.

6. *Take the high road.* There are many reasons to take offense, many opportunities to criticize, and many chances for conflict to erupt. A colleague is having a bad day and tosses off a thoughtless remark. Your boss is under pressure and takes it out on you. You feel overlooked or unappreciated or unheard. Some simple little remark gets blown completely out of proportion. All of these are perfect setups for trouble. If it escalates into a full-blown feud, it will be costly in terms of time, energy, productivity, and reputation. If you sense that a discussion is getting out of hand, cut it off at the pass. What if, just once, you observed the comment or the behavior or

the attitude in a very neutral, nonjudgmental way and then just let it go? If you feel you must do something, the single best thing you can do is *apologize,* even though you may not believe you were in the wrong.

7. *Don't play boss.* Theoretically you and your peer are on equal footing. Neither of you is in charge. It is simply good manners to couch requests in considerate, polite terms; but, with a peer, it is particularly important. You are not her boss, and you have no right to tell her what to do, under any circumstances. Besides that obvious observation, ordering people around can be hazardous to your career. If that's the kind of manager you would be, you may never get to be a manager.

8. *Don't cut people off.* Have you ever been in the middle of a sentence when someone blithely interrupted and started talking? Once is forgivable; but, if that sort of thing happens repeatedly, you will find yourself either talking much faster to get all the words in or getting annoyed enough to say, "Would you mind letting me finish?". Now, put the shoe on the other foot. If you hate to be interrupted, you can assume others do as well. Interruptions send a clear message that you aren't very interested in what the speaker is saying. You don't have to start talking to interrupt. You could simply look disinterested, watch the activity going on around you instead of giving your full attention to your colleague, take phone calls, allow someone to interrupt the conversation, or doodle. People who are truly interested in what they are hearing do not doodle. They make eye contact; they listen; they ask questions; and they respond to the answers.

9. *Watch your language.* Words have power. Yet most people toss them around with little thought about their impact or consequences. A big part of packaging your message is to think about the words you use before they just tumble out of your mouth. Some words are loaded, and people respond to them with great emotion or are hurt by them. If you are speaking about a peer and use words like *costly mistake, control freak, unacceptable behavior, incompetent,* and

a host of others, you may do irreparable harm to that person, not to mention to yourself. There are not too many rules to live by that begin with *never, never do this,* but here is one. *Never, never use a disparaging, derogatory, or demeaning term to refer to or describe another person.* Even if you are in a environment conducive to such language and "everybody does it," *never, never do it.*

10. *Think before you speak.* If you were angry at your boss you would certainly think twice before you gave her a piece of your mind. No matter how accepting this person may be, she is unlikely to enjoy being taken to task by a subordinate. If someone reports to you and you have something unpleasant to say to her, you will probably remain conscious of your role as a supervisor or manager and deliver your message with some degree of tact. But in the fuzzy ground in between, where you and your peers dwell, you may simply dispense with the thinking-twice rule and say whatever is on your mind. It takes a fairly solid relationship to withstand that kind of assault too many times. Even if your peer is your friend, it doesn't mean anything goes. Friendships have been known to suffer irreparable harm because of careless communication.

How to Earn and Keep Respect

If you have no power in a peer relationship, what *do* you have? "The only resources I have are my credibility and the respect I have tried to build over the years," observed Lois LaDriere in the introductory interview. "If they respect my judgment, if they feel I am fair, if they believe I know what I'm doing, they will listen to me." That, in a nutshell, is what this chapter is all about. If your coworkers respect your judgment, feel you are fair, and believe you know what you are doing, they will listen to you. They will cooperate with you. They will play on your team.

Respect, of course, must be earned. You can't beg, borrow, or buy it. It is earned by a consistency of intention, words, and actions. In other words, *everything* counts. Here are some of the things that count the most:

• *Be yourself, respect yourself, be true to yourself.* No one likes a phony, and people are smarter than you think. They see right through any performance to the real you. No matter how good an actor you are, you're bound to slip eventually and show your true colors. By the way, what's wrong with your true colors? If you look closely you might discover how much they become you. Respect, like charity, begins at home. If you don't show respect for yourself, why should anyone else? If you are constantly putting yourself down or letting other people run roughshod over you, those are sure signs of disrespect. One of Shakespeare's most frequently quoted lines is "to thine own self be true." That means don't cop out, don't behave in a way that isn't worthy of you, and do maintain your integrity at any cost.

• *Respect others—genuinely, obviously, consistently.* If *you* need respect, doesn't it seem logical that everyone else does too? Yet, why would someone grant you respect if you don't return the favor? This is a not a simple concept. If you honestly do not respect other people, that question may require some soul searching. If you don't start from the premise that every person on the planet deserves respect, simply because he or she is a human being, you have to ask yourself why. You can't fake this. If you feel another person is worthy of your respect, it shows; and if you don't, it shows too.

• *Be willing to say "I was wrong, I made a mistake, that was my fault, I apologize."* It is very difficult for some people to admit they were wrong or that when something went wrong it was because of their actions. The words, *I'm sorry* aren't even in their vocabulary. If you're wrong, you're wrong. It really is no big deal, and chances are it's not a secret either. If you messed up, what is so terrible about saying, *Whoops. I goofed?* Will you lose face? Must you be right all the time? Couldn't the other person be right just this once? And, if you did something you regret, will you choke on the words *I apologize?* It is not very likely. If these things are not in your repertoire, you might want to add them.

• *Assume everyone has something to teach you, and be willing to learn.* There are indeed lessons to be learned from every person you encounter. Sometimes they are profound lessons; other times, mundane. They may be taught by positive example or by behavior you would rather die than emulate. Sometimes what you learn is intentionally taught. A mentor takes you aside and counsels you; an expert shares his or her knowledge with you; an older person demonstrates the wisdom gained in the course of a long life. The important thing is to be open to the lessons all around you and to people you may never have thought of as your teachers.

• *Play fair, seek balance, try to see the other point of view, even if you have strong feelings.* If there are two points of view, and one of them is yours, how can you be certain that you are right and the other person is wrong? From where you're standing, of course, your perspective seems quite reasonable. From where she is standing, your colleague feels exactly the same way. Did you ever consider that no one is actually right or wrong and that you are just coming from two different worlds? Go back to *ask before you tell, listen before you speak.* This is one of the places to apply that advice. Try to find out what the other person feels and why. It won't be difficult. In fact, she may fall over from surprise that you even asked. You may or may not embrace her point of view, but at least you will have tried to grasp it. It's easier to play fair once you have done that.

• *Share the spotlight, give credit where credit is due, let others shine.* Just as you don't always have to be right, you don't always have to be the star. If you accomplish something and deserve the applause, by all means, accept it. If someone else accomplishes something, you should be the first in line to yell *Bravo!* It takes a big person to share the credit, the limelight, or the admiration; but that is exactly the kind of person who wins the respect of others. Here is another *never, never: Never, never take credit for something you did not do or an idea that wasn't yours.* That's called stealing.

• *If you say you are going to do something, do it. Consider it a contract.* Credibility means you come through. If you say you'll be there, you show up. If you promise to call, you call. If you offer to help, you are there with your sleeves rolled up. Your word is your bond, and your colleagues can count on it and you. There is no better way to earn respect.

Conclusion

"People skills" is a perfect example of business-eze. What is a *people* skill? How do you develop one, or do they come in clusters? Which ones are essential to professional advancement and which are optional? What if you are people-skill disadvantaged? Is there hope for you?

For lack of a better term, we seem to be stuck with people skills for now. What it means is the ability to interact and get along with humans. Perhaps nothing expressed it more eloquently than the report card we all received in the primary grades. Did you get good marks or bad marks in the box next to "Plays well with others"? Was that the beginning of a trend?

To play well with others, to get along, to cooperate means just what it always meant: be nice, share, don't fight, help your friends, don't call people names, and respect the rights of others. If you got it, then you have it now. Those are the essence of people skills.

CHAPTER FOURTEEN

Living With Anger and Conflict

Chip Planck has worked in the military, such large corporations as AT&T and Southwestern Bell, in small business enterprises, and now in his own entrepreneurial venture. He is a Viet Nam veteran who has witnessed and experienced anger at its most destructive and has spent many years coming to terms with this natural but potentially destructive emotion.

I think people often confuse anger with resentment. Anger is a perfectly normal emotion. If somebody does something that hurts you or violates your personal boundaries in some way, anger is an appropriate, healthy reaction. To *harbor* that anger—to store it and continue to replay it—that is resentment, and it can become damaging.

There is always going to be conflict, though it may or may or may not produce anger. Some people have trouble identifying anger, especially their own. They stuff it and internalize it, and it ends up hurting them. It comes out in various ways, though—as anxiety disorders; in the form of depression; and, many times, as serious illnesses.

The point is to be sensitive and recognize when something happens that does make you angry and to use a tool I call *detachment*. The idea of detachment is to examine what was said or done, try to figure out why you're angry about it, and consciously decide how to respond. By detaching in this way, you turn a negative situation into a positive one by responding in a calm, sane manner. Responding is not the same as reacting. Reacting is an emotional response. It doesn't involve much thinking. You say something or do something you may regret later. Responding is a planned action. You don't shoot from the hip; you *decide* how you will handle this situation. You are proactive rather than reactive.

If you find that a situation is going to cause you to react in a way that will make you feel uncomfortable, you should remove yourself as soon as possible. There is no circumstance in which you don't have a right to remove yourself. If you are in an angry confrontation with your boss, for example, first, don't react; and, second, head for neutral ground.

Some people are capable of doing this instantly. Most of us are not. All you have to say is, "Excuse me. I think it would be better to continue this discussion at a later time." Then you simply walk away. *How* you say it is important. When a person is angry and you speak in a soft, calm, even, measured manner, you not only defuse the anger, you put yourself in control. Anyone observing you from the outside will see you as rational and mature, as opposed to the person who is going crazy. If it is not your nature to respond this way, distancing yourself emotionally and physically is something you can learn to do.

Even though you have every right to detach and leave, you may not always have the discipline to do so, especially if you have a hair-trigger temper. If you lose control and make the mistake of reacting, you can't undo what has already been done. But you can recover by admitting that you were wrong and apologizing. You can simply say, "I'm sorry. I was out of line; but when you said so and so, it hurt me and this is how I interpreted it." By doing so, you are taking responsibility for your own response. Whether the other person admits he was wrong or not doesn't matter. What matters is *your* sanity and serenity.

Many people do what I call the J & R dance—justification and rationalization. Everybody has an excuse. It takes a strong person to take responsibility for his or her own actions. To do so suggests that you have spent some time thinking about what is really important—the big picture—and perhaps even visualized yourself responding calmly in an argument. If you play the scene over and over again in your mind, after a while you *become* what you have imagined. You're actually practicing for the moment when you'll need to respond automatically despite the emotions of the moment. The thought becomes the action.

When pilots are trained for combat, they rehearse the combat situation so many times that they automatically respond to real combat by doing exactly what they were trained to do. There are all kinds of powerful emotions that arise, but they have only a split second to react. They can't sit there locked in fear. They are conditioned to respond in a certain way. Their minds are disciplined to do what is necessary. They don't even have to think about it. They just do it.

Conflict is a normal part of life. You can't avoid it, so you have to get yourself to a place where you can resolve the situation and bring it to closure. Sometimes it's difficult to do that, and you need somebody you can trust with whom you can share and feel comfortable knowing that person will not violate your confidence.

Whenever we do something out of anger, we tear things down. We hurt the other person; but, more than that, we hurt ourselves. There's a proverb that goes, "A soft answer turneth away wrath." Every spiritual tradition has a similar saying. If you mediate on one of them for a while, you'll find that, eventually, it will replace your need to fight fire with fire when someone else is acting out of anger. Just because someone wants you to react, doesn't mean you have to. A careful, thought-out response is always best!

* * *

Emotions are part of our essential makeup. They are forces that propel us to some kind of action. We are bombarded with internal and external stimuli every moment, to which we respond with such emotions as joy, love, guilt shame, envy, or anger. Without emotions, we wouldn't really be able to cope with our environment. Yet, they are the source of a lot of problems in life.

The one we seem to have the most difficulty handling is *anger*—our own or someone else's when it is directed at us. If *we* get angry, we feel we have lost control and will never get it back. When *others* are angry with us, our feelings are hurt and our emotions are triggered, among them fear. Anger seems to suggest that violence is not far behind, although that is very rarely true.

Anger in the workplace is even more fraught with confusion, uncertainty, and anxiety. When someone is angry we feel the unwritten pact to *act* civilized has been broken, and there will be dire consequences. Of course, it depends on who is angry. If it is the CEO, he certainly won't suffer any dire consequences. If it is someone at a lower rank than the CEO—you perhaps, or your boss—there may be reason to feel anxious.

The point of this chapter is to focus on what you can do to weather the wrath of an angry, volatile person, especially if that person is your boss, and how to handle conflict, even if no one is actually yelling. First, you must understand the nature of anger and, second, some effective ways of dispelling it.

How to Handle Someone Else's Anger

• *Encourage the person to vent.* Emotions have to be released. You can't just let them sit there and hope they will go away. They won't. There are several seemingly helpful tools that actually prove completely ineffective in the face of anger. One is reason. Reason simply does not work as a way of diffusing emotion. In fact, it may make the situation worse. Distraction won't work either. Try talking to an angry person and keeping her attention. All she feels is her anger. If you do talk, she won't hear you. Don't try to change the subject or cheer her up, either. Instead, encourage her with questions, phrases, and gestures to keep her talking. Eventually, she will spend the energy that is fueling the emotion.

You have only one job—to get her to talk and release the venom. When someone is screaming at you or using abusive language or sarcastically putting you down, it *is* pretty difficult to remain calm, let alone focus on *her* emotion and *her* need to purge it. What you would probably prefer is for her to shut up, of course; but stand your ground. Rule number one is *let her vent.*

• *Help the person get in touch with angry feelings.* It is truly amazing how someone can stand in front of you, shouting, spewing forth a litany of expletives, and looking like he may have a stroke at any moment, yet *not know he is angry.* If you pointed it out he would deny it. *Other guys may pop off, but not me. I keep my cool,* is what he really believes. This is even more characteristic of the non-yeller, the person who, while not overtly angry, is seething inside. You may pick it up from nonverbal cues or just by being aware that he shows his anger in subtle, covert ways, such as being uncooperative, argumentative, or withdrawn.

In either case, you must make such people aware of what they are feeling. It won't be easy because all of us have developed very clever ways of hiding the feelings we don't like from ourselves. You can let the angry person vent until it is all out and then mention that he seems calmer and less angry. Or you can ask very direct questions that may help you get to the underlying problem.

Most people, of course, know they are angry when they are having a fit. They may fear losing control, but the advantages of unleashing their anger seem to outweigh the downside. Anger is a way of controlling others. Many angry bosses certainly know that and use it for just that purpose.

If control is not the reason, there are others you might explore. Does your boss subscribe to the militaristic mode: tell and do; I'm in charge; *attention*! Is she clearly an emotional person with mood swings all over the place? Does she get fired up and turned on, only to plummet into despair or anger? Any of those factors could be fueling her anger.

• *Take the anger in your stride.* When we are attacked, we either attack back or run away. That's called the *flight or fight response;* and, if you examine your own style, you can see which of these choices you usually make. Your angry boss or coworker may be expecting one or the other but will be thrown off stride if neither happens. If it is possible to observe the anger (it would probably be hard *not* to) and *do nothing,* you have a great advantage.

This person probably didn't plan to have a tantrum and would stop it if he could, but he can't. Emotions are not controllable; they are visceral. You can't tell him to stop being angry, but you can accept without judgment the emotion as it's happening. Try it the next time you are on the receiving end of anger.

Simply don't take a position on it. Think something like, *Oh, here comes another explosion,* and calmly watch it play itself out. Don't label it good or bad; don't criticize the other person or defend yourself. Just take it in your stride. Unless this person gets physical, which is unlikely, you will be perfectly safe. And it will dissipate. No one can rage forever.

• *Take steps to protect yourself.* A caveat to that advice is that, in some cases, the person might indeed lose control and "get physical." Then, you *are* at risk. If that happens, here are some ways to defend yourself and survive an attack.

- Stay at least two arm lengths away to avoid a possible punch. Back up slowly. If this person can't reach you, he can't hit you.

- Use natural obstacles. Keep a desk or chair between you and the threatening coworker. Move around so there is always something solid between the two of you.

- If you are standing, then sit down. Sitting is less confrontational. Keep your arms toward the aggressor with your palms up, which is interpreted as *peacemaker* body language.

- Keep talking in a calm, natural voice. For some reason, even berserk individuals seldom hit someone who is talking. Do not yell for help.

- Sound genuinely interested in finding out what the person wants or what her grievance is. Most rage is based on the feeling that one is not being listened to or taken seriously. Once you find out what the gripe is, repeat it in your own words.

- Give the person an out so that he will not feel there is nothing to lose by becoming violent. Tell him that it is natural to say things one doesn't mean when upset. This will make it clear to that person that discharge or severe discipline due is avoidable *if* the confrontation ends immediately.

- Build the person's self-esteem. Ego stroking is an excellent way to soothe raw nerves. Suggest that she is respected within the company and would be ruining a solid record because of a grievance that can easily be remedied.

- Point out what your colleague or boss can lose if he goes too far. Stress that the "too far" has not yet been reached; but, if necessary, security will be called. Point out that this situation can still be resolved peacefully and forgotten.

- Empathize. This is not the time to disagree with the person's position, no matter how unreasonable it may be. Stress that you would feel the same way if you were in her shoes. Agree that the "beef" is legitimate but that there is a better way to resolve it.

- Never threaten or lose your temper. The worst thing you can do is retaliate in kind. Raising your voice or cursing can enrage him to the point where, if he has a weapon, he may use it.

The Last Resort

You've read every book, tried every technique, gone for counseling, learned to meditate, and all for naught. You still have an out-of-control boss (it could be a coworker, but a boss is the toughest to handle); you are still shaking in your shoes; and you think you'll go mad if you have to live like this much longer. What are your options?

You could of course confront your boss, which would be difficult and risky and probably lead nowhere. You could go over his head to his boss, but that person may not speak to you unless you have documentation and have already tried confronting your boss. This is definitely a Catch 22. What is left are two alternatives: either you leave the company or you take formal steps to get help for your boss or to have him terminated.

Most companies do have formal grievance procedures. If yours does, find out from the human resources department what it is and how it works. Some companies take an informal approach; others do it by the book. Generally, the steps are straightforward, but there is no question that this will not be an easy process for you. Knowing it will be difficult. It only makes good sense to educate yourself; weigh the consequences of doing it versus not doing it; and be sure you have a knowledgeable, sympathetic person in your corner.

If you have done it the "right way," by filing a grievance and jumping through all the proper hoops, and that hasn't worked, you may choose to "go public." Of course, don't even consider doing that unless your can back up every word you say with facts and documentation.

Going public may mean whistle-blowing or exposing your boss to the media, the authorities, or the appropriate government agency. This is going to be time consuming, expensive, and stressful. If you haven't already left the company, federal laws prohibit the company or your boss from retaliating; but life could be tough if you choose to remain or return.

One other alternative is to take legal action, which is now supported by a number of laws on the books. If you decide to go this route, don't play do-it-yourself attorney. Seek professional help from someone who works in this field. And remember that this, too, could be a long, arduous process.

If none of these options sounds very encouraging, at least you have some. People file grievances and law suits all the time, and often they win. Don't give up without considering every aspect of your situation. Get the best advice you can, and be sure you are prepared for what is involved.

What to Do About Conflict

Conflict can range from an atmosphere of antagonism to outright war. Companies or work groups characterized by conflict are always a little tense, a little on edge. Sometimes conflict is quite obvious, like anger. Other times it is disguised, dressed up to look like friendly competition. But it is not friendly; and it takes its toll, especially if it simmers under the surface or goes on interminably. The ability to deal with conflict is a survival skill well worth cultivating because you may need it at any time in any situation.

Conflict in the workplace isn't always with a boss. It can take place between any two people or among any groups. Here are some questions you might ask yourself, no matter who is involved.

• *Does anyone have to be right or wrong?* So often in arguments both sides fight with everything in them because they have to be *right.* The implication is, if I am right, by definition, you must be wrong. The fact that this is not a logical conclusion doesn't occur to the adversaries. For one thing, there is frequently more than one right answer, one right solution, or one right approach. There may be dozens. With many to choose from, you may pick any one that fits your situation. That doesn't mean the others were wrong; it just means they were not a perfect fit. If you see a problem one way and your colleague sees it another way, you are bound to come up with different solutions. Perhaps both might work, or neither is completely off the mark, or there is a third idea no one has proposed yet. The attitude that no one has to be right or wrong cuts conflict off at the knees.

• *Is this an ego problem?* The conversation is getting out of hand. Tempers are rising. The other person is passionately defending her point of view. Yet, the whole thing doesn't really seem worth all this emotion. What's the problem here? Are you completely off base, or is this a control issue? Chances are you know this person pretty well, and you know what pushes her buttons. Ask yourself, does she have to be a star, get credit for this project, or run the show? Could it be that this has nothing to do with the nuts and bolts of the topic under discussion and everything to do with her personal needs? Does it matter to you who is in control or who gets credit? If it doesn't, simply giving up any formal leadership you may have should end the conflict. Unless you have the same needs, the real issue is guiding this project to a successful conclusion, not who is at the helm.

• *Are you a space invader?* Our sense of self isn't bounded by our skin. Most of us walk around inside a private, invisible bubble that represents the amount of airspace we feel we must have between ourselves and other people. You can easily observe this by gradually moving closer to another person. At some point he will begin, irritably or just absent-mindedly, to back away. Your bubble changes size, depending on your relationship with the other person. If it is your spouse, it's probably very small; if it is a stranger, it expands.

The normal distance we tend to want between ourselves and coworkers is about 18 inches. If you invade that 18 inches of some else's space, you trigger his flight or fight response. That bubble is sacred space and one of the unnoticed reasons for long-standing conflict in an office setting.

Misunderstandings can develop because people from different cultures handle space in very different ways. For two unacquainted North American adult males, the comfortable distance to stand for conversations is about two feet apart. South Americans and people from Arab countries prefer to stand much closer. Unless they are both aware of the other person's space needs, one or the other is going to experience severe discomfort. If space has never occurred to you, it is well worth keeping in mind the next time you find yourself in a conflict situation.

• *Is this argument even real?* Sometimes what looks like conflict isn't that at all. It is merely what linguist and author Deborah Tannen refers to as "ritual opposition" or efforts to probe the advantages and disadvantages of a particular idea under discussion. These discussions can get quite emotional as questions fly back and forth. It may feel like you are being attacked, personally, when actually it is just *your idea* that is being tested and kicked around. The purpose of ritual opposition is to defend your ideas, not yourself. For many women in business this is a learned response rather than a natural one. Taking the time and trouble to learn it, however, can propel you right up the career ladder. Not learning can have just the opposite effect.

• *Which should you believe: what you see or what you hear?* The answer is what you see, and here is why. What you hear is a verbal message, and what you see and sense is a nonverbal message. Nonverbal and verbal messages often contradict each other. When that happens, don't you usually believe what you *see* rather than what you hear? Picture this: You are talking to your boss, who insists she is listening and that you should continue. Yet, if, while you're talking, she is pulling on her jacket, organizing her briefcase, and checking her watch, do you really believe she's listening? Not on your life! As your mother probably told you, *Actions speak louder than words.*

Nonverbal listening doesn't even require the ability to hear. Those who are deaf or hearing impaired "listen"—often very effectively—through their senses of sight, taste, smell, and touch. Even though many of your own choices and decisions are based on information you take in through your other senses, you may not realize how much you depend on them and how much more accurate they are than words.

Is the other person lying? Sometimes, unfortunately, that is the case; but, more often, she is *incongruent.* If she says she's listening, she thinks she is. If he denies he is angry, he believes it. If the person insists she is calm and in control, but tension is radiating out of every pore, believe the tension.

• *Are you getting the straight scoop here?* On the other hand, don't get hung up on whether the verbal and nonverbal messages are the same or different and assume you are not getting the whole truth, nothing but the truth from your discussion partner. Chances are, under the best of circumstances, you aren't anyway. Though we all walk around with the inaccurate self-image that we are honest to a fault and always tell it like it is, both notions are false. Few people are honest to a fault; and most of us hedge, package, edit, delete, and massage what we say.

If you and your adversary have just had a knock-down, drag-out battle in order for you to get some information you want, and you finally get it, the *worst* thing you can do is question its veracity or accuracy. If you do, you'll never win another one.

• *Is there* anything *we agree on?* One of the first rules of successful negotiation is to find one single area that both parties can relate to and start from there. It could be that you both have a personal interest in getting this project completed or that the team will benefit from your efforts. It may be something obvious or obscure. Sometimes it comes down to the fact that you are both of the same gender or age or ethnic background or stage of parenthood—all pretty personal areas—and that one of those is all it takes to get the ball rolling. If you find one, use it because chances are there are more where that came from. The point is, if you are getting nowhere, arms folded across your chests, intractable, holding your ground, you could stay there for a long time. Who will this benefit? Surely, it will not help you, the other person, the department, or the company. Seek out that *one* thing you can both agree on, and get off the dime.

The Million-Dollar Skill: Assertiveness

In the face of wrath, bad behavior, lack of consideration, and conflict, there is one tool or skill that works across the board. The word is not a new one; it is *assertiveness.* Acting assertively has three parts: The first is standing up for your own rights and expressing what you believe, feel, and want. The second is doing that directly, honestly, and appropriately. And the third is respecting the rights of the other person while you are doing it.

We have been taught all through our school and business lives to express ourselves with caution, to carefully package what we say, and to be aware of the consequences of candor and directness. T*elling it like it is* not the way we are used to communicating. Why do it, then? Why fly in the face of years of conditioning and invest time and effort in learning to be assertive?

How many times have you walked away from a situation *without* getting what you deserved—like the raise or promotion you expected but didn't receive; or respect as an adult from your supervisor, instead of patronization; or even simple civility instead of a temper tantrum? You *deserve* to be fairly compensated and rewarded for good work. You *deserve* courtesy, respect, and good manners. When you learn to behave assertively, you stand a much better chance of getting what you deserve.

When you feel you're entitled to something and don't get it or when people treat you rudely or angrily, often you may feel that you were to blame in the first place. Maybe you didn't *really* deserve whatever it was you thought you did. So, one of the consequences of not getting what you feel you deserve in life is a bruised ego. Conversely, one of the benefits of assertive behavior—of standing up for your rights and asking for what you want in a direct, genuine manner—is improved self-esteem. Even when you don't get what you want, which is part of life, you are likely to feel better about yourself because you did something proactive about going after it.

Another consequence of not getting what you feel you deserve from someone is that something happens to your relationship with that person, especially if he is a friend or a colleague or your boss. If a salesperson is rude or a stranger cuts you off in mid-request, it may sting a little; but no real harm is done. But when the person you eat lunch with every day or the one you report to treats you badly, it's a different story. Whether you lash out or close up, either way, the relationship has sustained a wound.

How can being assertive change that? By preventing the wound from occurring in the first place. When you ask for what you want or express your feelings without apology or embarrassment, without attacking others in the process, your relationships will actually grow stronger.

How do you develop this million-dollar skill and make it part of your own behavior? You begin by getting a grasp of the key elements of assertiveness, which are: showing respect for yourself and for the other person, being direct, being appropriate, picking the right time to say what's on your mind, monitoring the intensity of how you say it, knowing the relationship you're dealing with, repeating yourself as often as necessary, and letting your body do some of the talking.

• *Showing Respect for Yourself and the Other Person*— Without self-respect, you would have no reason to be assertive. Responsible assertive behavior means valuing yourself, putting limits on what you're willing to do for others, realistically assessing what you can do and what you can't do, not blaming yourself when someone treats you badly or unfairly, and forgiving yourself for making mistakes. The other side of respect is giving it to others, which simply means honoring their rights as people. It does *not* mean deferring to their whims and wishes.

• *Being Direct*—Be direct in the way you deliver your message. Don't make excuses; don't use sarcasm. If you say what you mean, it leaves very little room for misunderstanding. Hinting, being indirect, and using sarcasm or insults are anything but direct or honest. Being honest means that what you say and how you say it accurately express your feelings, opinions, or desires. The truth doesn't have to hurt, if it's packaged with concern for the other person's feelings and in a way that will promote your own self-respect.

• *Being Appropriate*—Appropriateness encompasses many nuances, including when and where you choose to express yourself, how strongly you do so, how often you repeat it, who else is around, and your relationship with the other person. When and where you decide to be assertive does matter.

• *Picking the Right Time to Say What's on Your Mind*— Timing is everything. If you pick the right time and place and deliver your message assertively, you may get exactly the outcome you want. If you pick the wrong time and place, you will have shot yourself in the foot. It's probably a poor time or place when the other person is busy doing something else; when he is in the middle of a sentence, and you have to interrupt him to make your point; when you or she is in a hurry and won't have time to finish the conversation; when one or both of you are upset; when the event in question happened so long ago that no one but you remembers it; when the person you're talking to is clearly unresponsive to what you're saying; when there's no time to process what you have said; or, when there are other people around.

• *Monitoring the Intensity of How You Say It*—How *firmly* or *intensely* you make your statement helps underscore how much you mean it. Which of these examples is the most effective way of saying "no"?

- *Well, I'm pretty busy right now. I really don't think I have the time to do this ...*

- *I hope you won't take this wrong, but I'd just rather not get involved in your project. It's not my kind of thing.*

- *The project sounds very worthwhile, Sue, but I've made several other commitments for my time in the next few weeks. If I take on one more thing, I know I won't be able to do it justice. Thanks for asking me. But I really must refuse.*

• *Knowing the Relationship*—The relationship you have with the other person determines not only what you say but how you say it. What will suffice with a total stranger may be inadequate with a coworker. Saying *no* to a friend can be a real test of assertiveness because you don't want to jeopardize the relationship. How you would state your case to your boss will probably be quite different from the way you would do it with someone from another department. While, in each of these situations, assertiveness will pay off, *how much you say* will vary with the relationship.

• *Repeating Yourself*—Sometimes, even though you deliver your message in the right way, it doesn't get through. You may have to *repeat* it, perhaps more than once, and increase your intensity each time. While this is an effective way to make a point, it can also backfire if you overdo it. Another effective tool that can be overdone is the use of "I statements" to express your feelings. "I statements" keep the responsibility for your feelings and opinions with *you* and not with the other person.

• *Letting Your Body Do Some of the Talking*—The last element of assertiveness is *body language,* which is often more eloquent than words. It is a very important way of communicating because it conveys so much of what you are feeling. The first step in letting your body do the talking is to be aware of what it's saying. Passive, aggressive, and assertive behaviors all have their own body languages. You know them when you see them because body language is usually something that is observed, seen, or sensed, rather than described. In other words, you talk with your eyes, your face, and your gestures. Watch other people, and try to be conscious of the messages you are sending. Ask close associates for feedback and then accept it graciously.

Conclusion

"It's a jungle out there" is a line you have probably come across in your career. When you find yourself dealing with anger and conflict, it's an especially apt description. You wouldn't go on safari without the proper preparation and gear. Apply the same rules to the workplace. Sad as that advice may be, it is realistic. Naturally, you will not want to seek out unhealthy emotions and verbal attacks behind every desk and under every plant; but when you do come upon these little beasties, wouldn't it be nice if you were armed?

Bibliography

Acuff, Frank L. *How to Negotiate Anything With Anyone Anywhere Around the World*. New York: Amacom, 1993, 1997.

Aubuchon, Norbert. *The Anatomy of Persuasion*. New York: Amacom, 1997.

Deal, T. W. and A. A. Kennedy. *Corporate Cultures: The Rites and Rituals of Corporate Life*. Reading, Mass.: Addison-Wesley Publishing Company, 1982.

DuBrin, Andrew J. *The Breakthrough Team Player*. New York: Amacom, 1995.

Fritz, R. and K. Kennard. *How to Manage Your Boss*. Hawthorne, N.J.: Career Press, 1994.

Henig, R. M. and the Editors of *Esquire* magazine. *How a Woman Ages—Growing Older: What to Expect and What You Can Do About It*. New York: Ballantine/Esquire Press, 1985.

Kabat-Zinn, Jon, Ph.D. *Full Catastrophe Living*. New York: Dell Publishing, a division of Bantam Doubleday Dell Publishing Group, Inc., 1990.

Jakubowski, Patricia and Arthur Lange. *The Assertive Option*, Champaign, Ill.: Research Press Company, 1978.

Janis, Irving L. *Victims of Groupthink*. Boston, Mass.: Houghton Mifflin Company, 1972.

Naisbitt, John and Patricia Aburdene. *Megatrends 2000*. New York: William Morrow and Company, Inc., 1990.

Quick, Thomas, L. *The Persuasive Manager*. Radner, Penn.: Chilton Book Company. 1982.

Schaef, A. W. and D. Fassel. *The Addictive Organization: Why We Overwork, Cover Up, Pick up the Pieces, Please the Boss and Perpetuate Sick Organizations*. San Francisco: HarperSanFranscico, a division of HarperCollins Publishers, 1988.

Toropov, B. *The Art & Skill of Dealing With People*. Paramus, N.J.: Prentice Hall, a Simon & Schuster Company, 1997.

Toropov, B. *The Complete Idiot's Guide to Getting Along With Difficult People*. New York: Alpha Books, a Simon & Schuster Macmillan Company, 1997.

Williams, R., M.D. and Williams, V., Ph.D. *Anger Kills*. Harper Perennial, a division of HarperCollins Publishers, 1993.

Index